# The
# Arts of the Church

Edited by the
REV. PERCY DEARMER, M.A.

Masaccio]                                          [Mansell, Photo.

S. LAURENCE.   (See page 66.)

# The Arts of the Church

# SYMBOLISM OF THE SAINTS

BY THE
REV. P. H. DITCHFIELD, M.A., F.S.A.

*WITH FORTY ILLUSTRATIONS*

A. R. MOWBRAY & CO. LTD.
LONDON : 28 Margaret Street, Oxford Circus, W.
OXFORD : 9 High Street

First printed, 1910

# EDITOR'S NOTE

———

THE little volumes in the ARTS OF THE CHURCH series are intended to provide information in an interesting as well as an accurate form about the various arts which have clustered round the public worship of God in the Church of Christ. Though few have the opportunity of knowing much about them, there are many who would like to possess the main outlines about those arts whose productions are so familiar to the Christian, and so dear. The authors will write for the average intelligent man who has not had the time to study all these matters for himself ; and they will therefore avoid technicalities, while endeavouring at the same time to present the facts with a fidelity which will not, it is hoped, be unacceptable to the specialist.

# PREFACE

A STUDY of symbolism is essential
for the understanding of almost all
branches of ecclesiastical art, painting,
sculpture in stone or wood, and the architecture of various ages. It is shown on
the walls of churches, fonts, screens, miseri-
cords, carvings, pictures by great mediæval
artists, and enters largely into the sacred
art of all countries. It has, therefore, been
deemed advisable to include the subject of
" Iconography" in this series of the Arts of
the Church. The writer has endeavoured
to record the symbols of those saints whose
figures appear most frequently in churches
and in works of Sacred Art, and to give
such brief accounts of their lives and
legends as may account for the selection
of their symbols. The very limited space
at his disposal has, of course, prevented
any full treatment of the subject; but
the reader will probably find this book,
especially the indexes, sufficient to enable
him to recognize the identity of the figures

which he may meet with when studying
the beauties of churches or the paintings
of Old Masters.   The writer is indebted
to the works of many authors who have
toiled in the same field.   These are far
too numerous to be here mentioned.
Alban Butler's and the Rev. S. Baring-
Gould's *Lives of the Saints* have been used,
and Dr. Owen's *Sanctorale Catholicum*,
Mrs. Jameson's *Sacred and Legendary Art*,
Husenbeth's admirable work on *Symbolism*,
Hind's *Garner of Saints*, Hulme's *Symbolism
in Christian Art*, and Mrs. Arthur Bell's
valuable work on *The Lives and Legends of
Evangelists, Apostles, and other Early Saints*,
are some of the books which have been most
useful to him in his search for symbols and
their signification.   To the General Editor
of the series, Mr. Percy Dearmer, and to
the publishers, he desires to express his
cordial thanks for the great assistance they
have rendered in the selection of illustrations, and for much valued co-operation in
the preparation of this book for the press.

# CONTENTS

# LIST OF ILLUSTRATIONS

Plate 1.

THE VIRGIN AND CHILD SURROUNDED BY SAINTS.

(See page 15.)

# The Arts of the Church

# SYMBOLISM OF THE SAINTS

*⁂*

## CHAPTER I

### *Introduction*

FROM the earliest times it has been customary to adorn our churches with representations of the holy men and women who have been deemed worthy to rank among the Saints. The glorious company of the Apostles, the goodly fellowship of the Prophets, the noble army of Martyrs, live still in sculptured art, in curious painting, in glowing glass, and remind the faithful of their brave deeds, their awful sufferings, and of the crown that they have won. Art, the handmaid of Religion, teaches by the eye the holy lessons and sacred truths which the ear often fails to retain and convey to the heart and spirit.

In the early days of Christian Art it was usual to assign a certain peculiarity of form and personality to some particular saint. Correct portraiture, exact likeness, a photographic semblance, were, of course, unknown in Apostolic times. A conventional likeness was gradually given to each Apostle or Martyr or Confessor. Thus S. John is usually represented as a youth, S. Philip appears as an old man, S. Peter with a short, rounded beard, S. Andrew with a long flowing one. But it was difficult for the early artists clearly to distinguish a large number of persons ; hence it was found useful to assign to each an appropriate symbol, some object connected with the life or death of the saint, some sign by which his figure might be recognized. The symbol is not always the same. Artists in ancient, as in modern times, sometimes strove after originality. But the saint can generally be known by his symbol, and it may be convenient to modern painters, to those who visit picture galleries, or love to examine the details of old glass or mural painting, to record again these signs which custom and early art have bestowed upon the Apostles and Martyrs of the Church. Sometimes the figures in mural painting or window have entirely disappeared, but traces of the symbols remain, and enable us to determine what has been lost. Thus in the little church of Hitcham, in Buckinghamshire, there is some ancient stained glass, broken relics of curious and interesting designs ; but here and there the careful eye can see the figure of an ox, a lion, and an eagle, and can conclude that formerly there were some representations of the four Evangelists. The knowledge of symbolism is, therefore, of immense value to the antiquary and the student of Christian Archaeology.

The whole history of the principles and practice of symbolism in Christian Art is almost as vast as the stories of the lives of the saints. It is in the language of pictures. It takes some well-known object— a lamb, a dove, a lion, or a serpent—and teaches spiritual truths. How important a part it played in the days of ignorance can well be understood. Even heathen folk recognized its value, and Clement of Alexandria advised the Christians of his age to substitute for their pagan devises, engraved on stones and rings, certain Christian emblems such as the dove, a symbol of the HOLY SPIRIT, the Cross, the palm-branch of victory, the anchor of hope, and similar devices. Symbols were devised to represent the Blessed Trinity, the hand and arm and eye of GOD the FATHER ; the *Agnus Dei*, the Good Shepherd, the sacred monogram, IHS and XP, the first letters of JESUS and Christus, for the Incarnate SON ; while the Holy Dove or a roll or a book distinguish the

HOLY GHOST. The history of the nimbus, its varying form and shape, the symbolism of the colours used in ecclesiastical art, the story of the Cross and crucifix, of allegorical figures, of the symbolic use of animals and flowers, are all of the highest importance, and bear witness to the development of the ideas of Christian Art and to the spirituality, imagination, and ingenuity of those who devised this complex system of pictorial instruction and devout musings.

It is beyond the purpose of this book to treat of the whole subject of symbolism, and our main concern is only with that branch of it which concerns the emblems of the Christian Saints. The Old Testament patriarchs, prophets, kings, and saints are not forgotten in the chronicles of art. Abraham bears the knife with which he was prepared to offer his son Isaac to JEHOVAH. Noah bears a miniature ark, or the dove and olive-branch that signified the abating of the waters of the flood.   Aaron wears his priestly vestments, and holds in his hand a censer or a rod. In allusion to his being cast into the lions' den, Daniel has for his symbol the forest king, and sometimes a ram with four horns.   The Tables of the Law are borne by Moses ; Jonah bears a large fish or a ship, and Elijah a chariot, or a sword in his hand and a child near him.   Amos appears as a shepherd with sheep.   Elisha has a two-headed eagle on his shoulder ; Ezekiel a gate with towers in his hand. Isaiah bears the implement of his martyrdom, a saw.   Jeremiah bears a rush, and Joel is shown with a lion tearing him. Malachi has for his symbol an angel, and Zechariah the Temple in building.

But our chief interest is centred in the New Testament Saints, and in those of later days who have been deemed worthy of being accounted such.   The instruments of their martyrdom frequently suggested appropriate symbols.   The Holy Family, the companions of our LORD, the

Apostles, the holy women who followed the Saviour during His earthly life, the devoted men whose names are enshrined in Holy Writ, and who by their labours spread the Gospel light and laid the foundations of the Christian Church in many lands—all these are recorded in Christian Art by vivid paintings, and represented by symbols and emblems.

And as the cloud of witnesses increased in size, and the "noble army" enrolled new members under CHRIST's banner, new symbols were devised to mark each champion of the Cross, who by his life of sanctity, by his devotion even unto death, earned the glorious crown of martyrdom. Those thus honoured are only a few of that great company who have borne witness to the sincerity of their faith by the holiness of their lives.

"Many a name by man forgotten
Dwells around Thy throne most high."

The life-story of many is so interwoven

with legend and fabulous details that it is
difficult to guess the exact truth concerning them.    The identity of names has
caused no little confusion.    Thus legends
have confused the story of S. George the
Martyr, Patron Saint of England, with
George of Cappadocia, the Arian Bishop
of Alexandria, and have attributed some
of the events in the life of the heretical
bishop to the brave soldier-martyr.

To S. James the Greater has been
assigned the resuscitation of a man who
had been hanged, but this was originally told of a twelfth-century hermit,
S. Dominic de la Calzada, who mended
the road used by pilgrims to the shrine of
S. James of Compostella.    Hence the
confusion.

Sometimes it is not easy to discover on
what grounds canonization has been conferred.    It may be that in some cases
earthly judgements may not have been
altogether ratified by the Supreme Judge
who " trieth the reins and the heart."

*Plate* 2.

S. GEORGE. (See pages 8 and 164.)

But these considerations are beyond our present purpose. Nor are we specially concerned to separate reality from legend. The latter was not woven by the saint. He lived his life and did his duty, and perhaps died bravely with simple love and devotion to his Master. He is not responsible for the mass of strange stories and improbable traditions that the superstitious reverence and weird imaginations of future generations of Christians have invented and attached to his name ; and if he had been alive he would have been eager enough to declare their falseness. But the legend often has its uses ; it discloses the current beliefs, habits, and opinions of those who created it. It represents the ideas and aspirations of mediaeval Christianity. As an allegory it is often helpful in encouraging virtue, discipline, and bravery, and has doubtless urged many a lowly follower of Christ to imitate the example which the mythical history of the saint set forth.

We cannot record all their holy names or tell fully the events in their lives ; but it is our intention to mention those whom early artists most loved to depict, and to give so much of their history as may account for the selection of their symbol.

## CHAPTER II

### *The Holy Family*

CHRISTIAN thought first centres about the Holy Family at Bethlehem and Nazareth. The great forerunner of our LORD, the holy Baptist, constantly figures in the art of all Christendom, and Gospel History is closely followed. We see him clad in his coarse garment of camel's hair and bearing in his arms a lamb and a scroll with the words *Ecce Agnus Dei*, and a long staff with a small crosspiece near the end. His life and work are recorded in the Gospels, and need not be here repeated. In art his most frequent and almost universal symbol is a lamb, in allusion to his testimony concerning our LORD as

*Plate* 3.

Flemish School]          [Mansell, Photo.

THE MAGI.

(See page 19.)

the Lamb of God. Frequently the Lamb is placed on a book as in the rood-screen of Ranworth, Worstead, Burling-ham S. Andrew. A cross frequently is added, or a banner with cross. The figure of the holy Baptist is usually attired in the raiment of camel's hair and leathern girdle ; a lamb and locusts, his head on a dish, are some of his emblems. Paintings of the saint are in number legion.

Mrs. Bell truly says, " Scarcely a painter or sculptor of religious subjects, of whatever nationality, has failed to pro-duce one or more renderings of the fascinating theme, the Holy Family, but perhaps Raphael, Leonardo da Vinci, Correggio, Andrea del Sarto, Bernardino Luini, and Pinturicchio, have been most successful in interpreting the ideal character of the boy set apart from all others by his constant association with the Divine Child." All the other scenes of the saint's life are abundantly illustrated by numer-

ous artists—his preaching, the Baptism of
the Saviour, his martyrdom—and every
gallery of old masters bears witness to the
reverence they paid to the holy Baptist.

Around the memory of the Blessed
Virgin many legends have been woven, and
her assumption and coronation are depicted
by mediaeval artists quite as frequently as
the scenes of Gospel story. We see her
with her parents Joachim of Galilee and
Anna or Anne of Bethlehem, with Joseph
her husband and the Holy Child. A
branch of palm given to her by the angel
Michael from the ascended CHRIST to be
borne before her bier, roses and lilies of
the valley, her girdle that she let down
from heaven in order to convince the
unbelieving Thomas of her Assumption,
are some of her emblems. The Annunciation is one of the most frequent subjects
represented in art, and the old masters
loved to bestow upon the visit of the
angel Gabriel to the mother of our LORD
their highest reverence and their con-

summate skill. White lilies are the attribute of the Virgin, signifying her purity; these flowers are sometimes called annunciation lilies. In most pictures these flowers are introduced, as in Andrea della Robbia's bas-relief, and in many others. The rose also is a symbol, as in the painting of Benozzo Gozzoli in the National Gallery, in which roses and white lilies both appear. *Rosa Caeli*, and *Santa Maria dilla Rosa* are some of the titles of the Virgin. The snowdrop is also sometimes used. The *Golden Legend* remarks : "There be some people that aske a questyon why there stondeth a wyne potte with lilies between our Lady and Gabriel the Angell at her salutacyon. This is the cause, for our Lady conceyued by feyth."

S. Joseph has for his emblems a rod and lilies, and also a carpenter's plane, saw, and hatchet. The first is in allusion to the legend of the way in which the Virgin found her husband. The story states that

Luini] S. BENEDICT, S. JOHN BAPTIST. (See pages 12 and 97.)

[Brogi, Photo.

C

she had been in early life dedicated to GOD and lived with other virgins in the Temple. The High Priest ordered all of them who were of the proper age to be married, but Mary refused. The High Priest was in perplexity, but was advised by a voice from the Ark of the Covenant that all the unmarried men of the House of David should bring their rods to the altar, and the destined bridegroom's rod would bud, and on it the Spirit of GOD would descend. Although Joseph at first withdrew his rod, deeming himself too old to marry, he was chosen by GOD, and his rod budded, and the Holy Dove descended on it. Hence the symbol. We need not tell the curious story of the lives of the parents of the Virgin prior to her birth, their meeting at the golden gate of the Temple after their separation. This meeting is depicted in the Salisbury Missal of 1534. S. Anne appears in many works of art, teaching her child to read, offering fruit to the Infant JESUS, her chief emblems being a triple crown and a book.

Associated with the Holy Family are the Magi, whose visit to the Infant Saviour has been the favourite subject of inspired artists, and is recorded in altar-pieces, mural decorations, medals, and sculpture. The Wise Men are always three in number, and are represented as kings in fulfilment of the prophecy, " The Kings of Tarshish and of the Isles shall bring presents : the Kings of Sheba and Seba shall offer gifts. Yea, all kings shall fall down before Him : all nations shall serve Him." Tradition assigns to them names and a conventional aspect. The aged Gaspar has a long grey beard ; Melchior, a man in the prime of life, has a short beard, and Balthazar is a young beardless man. Sometimes the last is depicted as a negro, symbolical of the race of Ham. The gifts—gold, frankincense, and myrrh —according to the sequence of Hereford Cathedral, " mystically show that He to

Whom they offered gold was King, to Whom incense priest, by the myrrh is shown His burial. Let us offer to Christ in deed what the kings offered in figure. Let us examine our minds, and there is gold on the altar. Let us mortify our offences, and so myrrh is offered ; to the mysterious grace of virtues belongs the best incense of Saboea."

## CHAPTER III

### *The Apostles*

THE evolution of the symbols of the
Apostles possess many features of
supreme interest. We see them represented first as twelve lambs, with our
LORD as a sheep in their midst, with
a nimbus about His head. Then they
appear as venerable men, very similar in
appearance.

Legendary history tells of the origin
of the Apostles' Creed, how they all met
together and, inspired by the HOLY
GHOST, each one uttered an article of
the Creed. Early artists seized upon this
idea, and represented each Apostle holding
in his hand a scroll, on which was inscribed
the article he had uttered. The following

is the list of the Apostles with their inscribed scrolls :—

S. Peter—" I believe in GOD the FATHER Almighty."

S. John—"And in JESUS CHRIST His only SON our LORD."

S. James the Greater—" Who was conceived by the HOLY GHOST, born of the Virgin Mary."

S. Andrew—" Suffered under Pontius Pilate, was crucified, dead, and buried."

S. Philip—" He descended into hell."

S. Thomas—" Rose again the third day."

S. Bartholomew—" Ascended into heaven, and sitteth on the right hand of GOD the FATHER Almighty."

S. Matthew—" From thence He shall come again to judge the quick and the dead."

S. James the Less—" I believe in the HOLY GHOST."

S. Simon—" I believe in the holy Catholic Church."

S. Jude or Thaddeus—" In the forgiveness of sins."

S. Matthias—" In the resurrection of the body, and the life everlasting."

This is the usual order of the scrolls that are attributed to each Apostle, but there are sundry variations which need not now be particularized. Sometimes the number varies. In some pictures, frescoes, and mosaics Judas is not numbered with the

*Plate* 5.

Rubens]

[Anderson, Photo.

S. PAUL.

(See pages 24 and 26.)

Twelve, while in others we see S. Paul, S. Matthias, and S. Barnabas. The instruments of their martyrdom furnish additional symbols. S. Andrew carries the **X**-shaped cross that bears his name, and on which he was crucified. S. Bartholomew bears a knife, with which he was flayed alive. S. James the Less has a fuller's pole; S. Jude, a knotted club; S. Matthew, a hatchet; S. Simon, a large saw; S. Thomas, a lance; S. Philip, a long staff or pillar, from which he was hanged; S. Matthias, a battle-axe; S. Paul, a sword; Judas carries the money-bag that caused his covetousness and fall; S. John has a cup, from which issues a snake, to which symbol we shall allude later on. S. Peter bears the keys, in allusion to the words of our LORD, and also has a cock at his side, a memorial of the denial of CHRIST. By this means did the early artists distinguish the Apostles of our LORD, and we can trace the development of their artistic portraiture from the art of the catacombs, the early mosaics at Ravenna and Rome, to the wonderful conceptions of Andrea del Sarto, Raphael, Leonardo da Vinci, Paolo Veronese, and other great artists of later times.

We will try to discover some further details of their symbols. Foremost among the Apostles was Simon, surnamed Peter, whose life stands out conspicuously in the Gospels and the Acts, and who ever obeyed his LORD's command, "Feed My sheep." Church history tells of his labours at Antioch, of his foundation of the Church at Rome, and of his martyrdom under Nero, being crucified with his head downwards. Many stories are told of his life and miracles, and no Apostle appears more frequently in artistic representations. All the great painters of old have portrayed the Prince of the Apostles. His principal emblem is a key in his hand, in allusion to the saying of the Saviour, " I will give unto thee the keys of the kingdom of heaven." Sometimes two keys are given,

combined with a church, or a cross, or
a book. Guido's painting in the Pitti
Palace shows the saint weeping, with a
cock crowing near him. The rood-screen
at Blofield represents him in chains in
prison. Raphael painted him as meeting
our Saviour on the Appian Way, a work
which is now in the Vatican, where also is
Giotto's painting of S. Peter crucified with
his head downwards.

S. Peter and S. Paul are often represented together. The symbol of S. Paul
is a sword, the instrument of his death,
and also a fit attribute of one who
wielded so well the sword of the Spirit.
Sometimes two swords are given as his
symbol. A book is also used, and
a serpent, in allusion to his miraculous
escape from the bite of a snake at
Melita. Again, the phoenix and palm-
tree are not unusual emblems, showing
forth the teaching of the saint as regards
the Resurrection. The catalogue of the
paintings and painters of scenes from the

*Plate 6.*

S. PETER.
(See pages 24-26.)

life of the great Apostle, and of S. Peter, who is so often represented with him, would take many pages ; and from the earliest times to the present day great artists have striven to tell again and again the story of the devoted lives of these saints, to whose labours the Church of CHRIST owes so much.

The life of S. James the Greater, or the elder, is told in the Gospels, and his martyrdom in the Acts of the Apostles, by order of the cruel Herod. He was one of the favoured three who were allowed to witness some of the secret and most sacred scenes in our LORD's life. Spain claims him as its Apostle and its patron saint. On account of his mission to Spain he is often represented in art with the symbols of a pilgrim, with staff and shell and wallet, as on many English rood-screens. Christian legend states that the body of the saint was miraculously conveyed to Spain, where in the struggle with the Moors, he aided the Christians by appearing in battle and gaining for them the victory. Carreno de Miranda painted him riding on a white charger conquering the Saracens, and there are numerous other pictures of the saint in military garb. Molanus and others give him a sword as an emblem, that being the instrument of his martyrdom. The whole story of his life is told by Andrea Mantegna in some frescoes at Padua.

No words are needed to describe the intimate relations between the Saviour and "the disciple whom JESUS loved," as revealed in the Gospel narrative. Of the three festivals, which follow the feast of the Saviour's birth, well does our great English Church poet, John Keble, sing :

> "On the King of Martyrs wait
>   Three chosen bands, in royal state ;
> And all earth owns, of good and great,
>   Is gathered in that choir."

S. Stephen, a martyr in will and deed ;
S. John a martyr in will, but not in deed ;

the Holy Innocents, martyrs in deed but not in will, are the representatives of the three kinds of martyrdom.    S. John's witnessing for CHRIST was life-long, until at length he died in peace at Ephesus at the advanced age of nearly 100 years. Tradition states that at Ephesus he wrote his Gospel and Epistles, and that he was sent to Rome by order of the Emperor Domitian, and outside the Latin Gate was scourged and thrown into a caldron of boiling oil.   GOD preserved His servant, and he suffered no ill effects; he was then banished to Patmos in the Ægean Sea, and there wrote his Book of the Revelation.   Many legends cluster round the saint, the beloved disciple, which need not be recorded here.   His usual emblem is the eagle, which is seldom absent.   On some English rood-screens he has a cup with a serpent issuing from it.   This alludes to the attempted murder of the saint at Rome when he was ordered by Domitian to drink a cup containing

*Plate* 7.

S. JAMES.   (See page **28**.)

poison, or to some attempt on the part
of his enemies to poison him with sacramental wine. The serpent that issued
from the cup is said to have died at his
feet. A palm, a scroll, and an eagle are
his symbols in the statue of the saint at
Exeter Cathedral. Perugino painted him
with an eagle hovering above his head,
and Raphael depicted him mounted on an
eagle. Lucas V. Leyden painted the saint
writing the Apocalypse in the Isle of
Patmos, to which scene is added in a
MS. Book of Hours the devil upsetting
his ink-bottle. In the National Gallery
there is a painting of the saint depicted as
an old man attired in Mass vestments
lifted to heaven by the Saviour out of his
grave at the foot of the altar at Ephesus.
There are countless pictures of the
Apostle.

SS. Philip and James, without any particular reason, are commemorated on the
same day, May 1st, and appear together
in art. The Gospels tell their story.

Church traditions state that S. Philip preached the sacred truth in Phrygia and Galatia, and that he was crucified at Hierapolis by the priests of the god Mars. He had incurred their wrath by commanding in the Name of the LORD a serpent which they worshipped to leave their idol temple. The evil beast could not withstand the power of the uplifted cross, and withdrew itself from the temple. The enraged priests seized the Apostle, and crucified him with his head downwards. The legend of the serpent is depicted in the Church of S. Maria Novella, at Florence, by Lippi, together with other scenes from the saint's life, and also in the *Die Attribute*. When CHRIST fed the famished multitude, He said to Philip, " Whence shall we buy bread that these may eat ? " Hence a basket with bread, or two or three loaves, are symbols of the saint. On several English rood-screens he is so represented. The instrument of his martyrdom is also his symbol, a

D

T-shaped cross as in the glass window of Fairford Church, the coins of Brabant, and the paintings of Pietro Perugino and Mathias Grünewald. His crucifixion with his head downwards is shown on the bronze gates of S. Paul's, at Rome, and in the Church of S. Maria, in Trastevere. Albert Dürer gives as his symbols a cross and a book, and in *Le Tableaux de la Croix* (Paris : F. Magot, 1651) he has a cross in his left hand and money in his right. His association with S. James the Less has often led artists to depict them together.

Modern authorities state that there has been much confusion between James the Less, or the younger, and James the LORD's brother. According to the older interpretations S. James the Less, who is commemorated with S. Philip, was the Bishop of Jerusalem, and the writer of the Epistle, and with that we may here content ourselves. The Book of the Acts of the Apostles describes the Great Council in Jerusalem over which he presided. He

*Plate 8.*

Rubens]                                    [Anderson, Photo.

S. PHILIP.

(See pages 32-34.)

was beloved by the Jews, but was martyred in the reign of Nero. He was flung from the wall of the city, stoned and beaten by the populace, until at length a fuller with a club ended his tortures. Thus a fuller's club is the usual emblem of the saint, and appears on many English rood-screens and some fonts. For the same reason S. James is always esteemed as the patron saint of fullers. Scenes from his life are depicted in the frescoes of the Chapel of SS. James and Christopher in the Church of the Eremitani, at Padua.

We will refer to S. Matthew and his emblems in the chapter on the Evangelists.

SS. Simon and Jude, after the dispersion, are said to have worked together in Palestine, and afterwards at Babylon, where they were martyred. S. Simon was sawn in two, and S. Jude crucified. S. Simon's emblems are a saw, a fuller's bat, a fish in his hand or on the leaves of a book, two fishes, or an oar. S. Jude has for his symbols a boat, a child with a boat, a boathook, a carpenter's square, a fuller's bat, a ship with sails, a club, halbert, and inverted cross. In the Fairford windows he is shown carrying loaves and a fish.

The first-called Apostle of our LORD, S. Andrew, is often mentioned in the Gospels. We see him as a fisherman on the Sea of Galilee, and called to be a fisher of men. He preached in Scythia, Cappadocia, and Bithynia. He is the patron saint of Russia, and is said to have founded a church at Constantinople and to have died at Patras. The cross on which he suffered was shaped in the form of the letter **X**, although in some representations it is **V**-shaped, as on the bronze gate at S. Paul's Church, Rome. He hailed the cross with the words, " All hail, cross, which art consecrated by the Body of JESUS CHRIST, and wert adorned with His members as with pearls. . . . Take me hence and restore me to my Master."

His usual emblem is the cross saltire,

which he leans upon, or holds in his hand. Thus he appears on several English rood-screens. Sometimes a fish-hook is used as his symbol. Murillo's painting of the saint's martyrdom (Madrid Gallery) is considered his masterpiece, and scenes from S. Andrew's life appear in the Sistine Chapel, and in the church of the saint at Rome.

Of S. Bartholomew little is recorded in the Gospels. He is supposed to be identical with Nathanael, and after the dispersion of the Apostles he preached the word in India, Phrygia, and Armenia, where he suffered martyrdom, being flayed alive and crucified. On several English rood-screens he is shown with a flaying-knife in his hand, which also is his emblem in the Delamere brass at St. Albans. A knife and a book are often given as the symbols of the saint, and there is a painting at Nôtre Dame, Paris, showing the saint healing a princess of Armenia. He is sometimes represented bearing his skin

*Plate* 9.

Rubens]                              [Anderson, Photo.

S. BARTHOLOMEW.

(See pages 24 and 38.)

on his arm, and he appears in several
groups of saints, as in the marriage of
S. Catherine by Fra Bartolommeo.

Of the "doubting" Apostle, S. Thomas,
Church history tells that he preached the
Faith in India and the Eastern lands.
Many legends cluster around his memory,
of his wondrous preaching; and when the
Portuguese missionaries first visited India
they found many Christians who were
deemed to be the descendants of those
whom S. Thomas converted.   It is believed
that he was martyred at Meliapur, on the
coast of Coromandel, being slain with
spears.   Some traditions point to Edessa
as the place of his martyrdom.   His usual
emblem is a spear or lance, as shown on
several English rood-screens.   Raphael
depicted him with a carpenter's square as
his symbol, and he is the patron saint of
architects and builders.   This is in allusion
to the legend that he was sent by CHRIST
to Gondoforus, King of the Indies, to
build a palace, which that king required.

It was no earthly palace that S. Thomas would build, but "a house not framed by hands eternal in the heavens." The money which the king gave him for building he gave to the poor, and for his pains was cast into prison. A dying brother revealed to the king the nature of the palace which the saint was destined to build, and the king was converted to Christianity and assisted the saint to build the spiritual house, the Church of CHRIST, in the realm of the Indies.

The scene in the upper chamber, when the Saviour convinced the doubting Apostle of His Resurrection, has often been depicted by the great masters, Angelo Gaddi, Luca Signorelli, Luini, Rubens, and others. Raphael painted the saint receiving a girdle from the Blessed Virgin at her Assumption, and Fra Bartolomeo, Molanus, Sodoma, and others have also depicted the legend, which tells that S. Thomas, being absent when the Virgin died, showed the same unbelief which he had manifested with regard to the Saviour. So the Virgin appeared to him in glory, and presented to him her girdle. This girdle is one of the emblems of the saint.

Holy Scripture tells how S. Matthias was elected in the place of the traitor to complete the number of the twelve Apostles. Dorotheus writes that he preached the Gospel in Æthiopia, about the haven called Hyssus and the river Phasis, unto barbarous natives and ravenous of flesh, and that he died at Sebastopolis, where he was buried nigh the temple of Sol. Others state that he preached first in Macedonia, and afterwards in Judaea, where the Jews stoned him and afterwards beheaded him with an axe, after the Roman manner. Hence a battle-axe, sometimes a sword or hatchet, appear as symbols of the saint. Other supposed instruments of his death sometimes are shown, such as a cross, a spear, or a club—the artists not having been fully acquainted with the traditional story of his martyrdom. The

*Plate* 10.

Murillo]

MARTYRDOM OF S. ANDREW.
(See pages 24 and 37.)

axe, either in the form used by wood-
men, or the military weapon, seems to
be the more correct symbol.   Hence
carpenters have chosen S. Matthias as
their patron.

## CHAPTER IV

### The Four Evangelists

THE symbols of the Evangelists are
many and varied. In the earliest
representations we find no attempted
portraiture of SS. Matthew, Mark, Luke,
and John, save of the first and last as they
appear among the Apostles. The Evangelists are only depicted by scrolls that
bear their names. Then a pleasing fancy
exhibited them as four streams issuing
from the Lamb and watering the thirsty
hearts of the nations. They are the rivers
that watered Paradise—Pison, Gihon,
Hiddekel, and Euphrates—and turned
the barren earth into a new Paradise by
the message of the Gospel which they
proclaimed. But the usual emblems of

the Evangelists are the four symbolic creatures : the angel, lion, ox, and eagle, derived from the record of the vision of the prophet Ezekiel. Bishop Wordsworth wrote thus of these mystical symbols :

" The Christian Church, looking at the origin of the four Gospels, and the attributes which GOD has in rich measure been pleased to bestow upon them by His HOLY SPIRIT, found a prophetic picture of them in the four living cherubim, named from heavenly knowledge, seen by the prophet Ezekiel at the river of Chebar. Like them the Gospels are four in number ; like them they are the chariot of GOD Who sitteth between the cherubim ; like them they bear Him on a winged throne into all lands ; like them they move wherever the Spirit guides them ; like them they are marvellously joined together, intertwined with coincidences and differences, wing interwoven with wing, and wheel interwoven with wheel ;

*Plate* II.

Rubens]                                    [Anderson, Photo.

S. MATTHEW.

(See pages 24 and 50–52.)

like them they are full of eyes, and sparkle
with heavenly light ; like them they
sweep from heaven to earth, and from
earth to heaven, and fly with lightning
speed and with the noise of many waters."

It is unnecessary to inquire as to the
origin of these mysterious figures, but the
prophet seems to imply that they were
similar to the weird forms of Assyrian
sculpture which he had seen when he was
a captive by the river Chebar. We see
them again in the Apocalyptic Vision of
S. John the Divine at Patmos, recorded
in the Book of the Revelation. A lion,
a calf, a creature whose face was human,
and a flying eagle are the descriptions
which are therein recorded. From these
visions the symbols of the Evangelists are
doubtless derived.

The application of each to one of the
writers of the Gospels is beset with diffi-
culty, and various reasons are assigned
for the interpretation of the meaning of
the symbol. The angel with a man's face

denotes S. Matthew because he chiefly dwells in his Gospel on the human nature of our LORD. The lion of S. Mark testifies to the fact that that Evangelist proclaims very distinctly the royal dignity of CHRIST, the lion being the king of beasts. It is also a symbol of the Resurrection, and as S. Mark dwells most fully on the rising again of our LORD, for this reason the emblem may have been assigned to him. Legendary natural history states that young lions are born dead, but when their sire breathes on them on the third day after their birth, they come to life. Hence the association of the king of the forest with the Resurrection. The ox or calf was used in Jewish sacrifices, and this symbol was assigned to S. Luke as he dwells particularly on the sacrificial aspect of our LORD's Atonement, and on His Divine Priesthood. The eagle soars heavenwards and can gaze unflinchingly at the glowing orb of day, and is a fitting emblem of the

Evangelist and Apostle S. John, who bears us as on eagles' wings to behold the majesty and divine nature of CHRIST, to know the Incarnate Word Whom he revealed to men, and to comprehend the higher and sacramental teaching of Him Who is the Word and Wisdom of GOD. Other meanings have been assigned to these mysterious figures, such as the Incarnation, the Death, Resurrection, and Ascension of CHRIST, or the nature and offices of the Saviour, the Man, the King, Priest, and GOD. But these are later developments and interpretations of the mysterious figures.

As the writer of the first Gospel S. Matthew is constantly represented in art. An angel holding an ink-horn or inkstand is a constant emblem. On many English rood-screens he appears holding a money-bag or a square money-box, in allusion to his office of tax-gatherer. After the dispersion of the Apostles he preached the Gospel in Egypt and Æthi-

*Plate* 12.

Donatello]                    [Alinari, Photo.

S. MARK.   (See pages 49 and 52.)

opia, and is said by some to have been
martyred, being slain by a halbert, or
battle-axe, which also are his emblems.
A tall cross of wood is given on his
symbol in the Fairford windows, and a
**T**, probably meant for a carpenter's
square, is also one of his emblems. He
is sometimes shown leaning on a short
sword. "From whence He shall come
to judge the quick and the dead," is the
portion of the Apostles' Creed said to
have been contributed by S. Matthew,
and this is sometimes depicted on a scroll,
or engraved on a banner. The calling of
S. Matthew is a very favourite subject,
and was painted by Pordenone (Dresden
Gallery), Ludivico Caracci, and many
other masters, and the feast at his house
has been equally celebrated, notably in
the immense painting by Paolo Veronese
in the Academy at Venice.

Holy Scripture tells of John Mark, the
son of Mary, and sister's son of Barnabas.
In his mother's house the infant Church

at Jerusalem was nurtured. We see him
the constant companion of S. Peter, who
inspired his Gospel, and sent him to
Alexandria, where he founded the bishopric, and suffered martyrdom at the hands
of the priests of Serapis, who dragged him
by a rope to Bucolia until he died, the
rocks being stained with his blood. As
one of the four Evangelists he stands
conspicuous in artistic representations.
The lion is his usual emblem, for reasons
which we have already given. Other
emblems of this Evangelist are a pen,
ink-horn, and a scroll, with the words,
*Pax tibi, Marce, Evangelista Meus*, which
are said to have been spoken by our
LORD to the martyr in his prison. It
would be impossible to record here a
tithe of the representations of the saint.
His body was conveyed to Venice in 815
A.D., and placed in the Cathedral of S.
Mark, which was then rising; and there
we see numerous artistic presentments of
the saint in mosaic, sculpture and painting,

and the early coinage of Venice preserves his memory. The story of his martyrdom is told on the old bronze gates of a church at Rome, and in many other works of art, and many legends of his life are commemorated.

Genius has offered an unfading garland at the feet of the Evangelist S. Luke, the beloved and faithful companion of S. Paul, "the beloved physician," and skilful artist, the patron saint of artists and doctors. Some used to tell how the saint received the Gospel from the Virgin, whose portrait he painted. Several works attributed to him are in existence. Many painters have represented him taking the portrait of the Virgin. This portrait and the ox are his chief emblems, in addition to painting materials, a book and a pen. Molanus shows him as "the beloved physician." Tradition states that he was one of the two disciples who met our LORD on the way to Emmaus; and Titian, Rembrandt, and other masters have painted

*Plate* 13.

Correggio]

S. JOHN THE EVANGELIST.

(See pages 24, 30 and 49.)

him meeting our LORD, or recognizing
the Saviour at supper.

The emblems of S. John the Evangelist have already been enumerated in
the account of S. John, the "beloved
disciple," the Apostle of our LORD.

## CHAPTER V

### Some Saints of the First Century

CHRISTIAN Art loves to dwell on the memories of those who were near and dear to the Saviour, and we will now think of those saints who lived in the time of our LORD or immediately succeeded Him. Foremost among the friends of JESUS were the family at Bethany, Martha, Mary, and Lazarus.

Art has always recognized that S. Mary of Bethany was identical with S. Mary Magdalene, the penitent who washed the feet of the Saviour with her tears and wiped them with the hairs of her head. Painters, in accordance with the ancient belief of the Church, have loved to depict her with long, flowing, golden hair, kneeling at the feet of JESUS, and in the final

scenes of our LORD's life she is ever
present ; and all the greatest painters—
Corregio, Fra Bartolommeo, Andrea del
Sarto, Perugino, and countless others—
have represented her in attendance upon
the Saviour.

Another group of pictures represents
the expulsion of Mary, Martha, Lazarus,
with S. Maximian, in a boat without oars,
and their arrival at Marseilles, where
Lazarus became bishop, and S. Maximian
Bishop of Aix. There S. Martha van-
quished a dragon with holy water and the
power of the Cross, and led it captive with
her girdle, until it was slain by the people.
She gained many converts to the Faith by
her preaching, and she is said to have
raised a drowned man to life. The episode
of the dragon appears in many pictures,
and Annibale Caracci gave as her emblem
a holy water-vessel and asperges with a
dragon at her feet. Her attention to her
household duties is signified by a ladle and
keys at her girdle. While Martha was

*Plate* 14.

Fra Angelico] [Brogi, Photo.
S. MARY AND S. MARTHA. (See pages 57 and 58.)

preaching at Aix Mary retired to a cave
and spent her days in meditation and
communion with her LORD.    There is
a story of her preaching to King René of
Marseilles, and of the birth of his son, of
his journey to Palestine, the death and
resurrection of his wife, and the saving of
his boy.    At the Musée de Cluny S. Mary
is shown preaching to the king.    Very
numerous are her emblems.    A box of
ointment in her hand is the most frequent,
as shown in many English rood-screens.
Instead of the casket sometimes she holds
a vase, as in the painting of Caracci.    On
the Denton church chest she appears holding a boat and an open book, in allusion
to her journey across the sea.    Her last
years of meditative life are depicted by
many artists.    Guido Reni shows her
holding a crucifix with an open book
before her with a skull upon it.    Murillo's
famous painting shows her with a skull.
In the baptistery at Florence she appears
standing covered with her flowing hair.

It is impossible to refer to a tithe of the paintings which record her symbols and commemorate her life.

Lazarus is clad in episcopal robes, though it is doubtful that he ever became Bishop of Marseilles. His symbol is a bier, in token of his being raised from the grave by our LORD ; sometimes he appears wrapped in grave-clothes, and also has a boat for his emblem in memory of his voyage. He is said to have been martyred at Marseilles.

You can always see in pictures of the Passion a woman holding a veil or handkerchief. This symbol denotes S. Veronica, who, according to the beautiful legend, beholding the Saviour on His road to Calvary, struck with compassion for His sufferings, wiped His bleeding brow with the veil or napkin that was on her head, and received it back with the miraculous impress of the Saviour's face. Some have said that she was the woman whom He healed of the issue of blood. Many legends have clustered around her name, but these we cannot record now. The veil is still at the Vatican.

Another figure that is always seen in the Descent from the Cross is that of Joseph of Arimathæa. He was exiled with the family of Bethany, and we should like to believe the early legend that he wandered through Gaul to Britain and founded our first Christian church at Glastonbury. His pilgrim's staff rooted itself and blossomed into the Holy Thorn, and he brought with him the spear that pierced the Saviour's side and the cup used at the Last Supper. This cup and his staff are his symbols, the former becoming known as the Sangreal, which forms a striking feature of the Arthurian legends.

S. Barnabas, "the son of consolation," the beloved companion of S. Paul in his missionary journeys, was martyred at Cyprus. The fact that the people of Lystra deemed him to be an incarnate Jupiter seems to prove that he was of a noble and commanding appearance.

Plate 15.

S. STEPHEN.

(See page 29.)

*Plate* 16.

Signorelli]  [Hanfstaengl, Photo.

S. MARY MAGDALENE.  (See page 57.)

He was either stoned or burnt to death. When his body was discovered, the Gospel according to S. Matthew, copied by his own hand, was found lying on his breast. This Gospel often appears as his symbol, as in the painting by Bonifazio, and also the instruments of his death—stone, or flames and a stake. A statue at Exeter Cathedral shows him with an open book and a staff as his symbols.

Associated with the above saints is S. Timothy, who was slain by the priests of Diana at Ephesus. They stoned him and beat him with clubs. These instruments have been chosen as his symbols. Stones also are the attributes of the proto-martyr S. Stephen, who is usually depicted as a young deacon in his dalmatic, and holding stones in his robe, or in a napkin, or in his hand. He usually bears a martyr's palm. His body was ultimately removed to Rome and buried in the Church of San Lorenzo, in the same tomb with S. Laurence. Hence in art the

F

two martyrs are often coupled together, though they lived two centuries apart.

The memory of the heroic S. Laurence, who was also a deacon, is venerated throughout Christendom. When the treasures of the Church were demanded of him, he told the prefect that he would produce them in three days, and on the third day presented a company of poor people, and said, " These are the treasures of the Church of CHRIST." The prefect ordered him to be roasted to death on an iron frame resembling a gridiron. He bore his sufferings with amazing fortitude, and even taunted his persecutors with the words, " One side is roasted ; turn me and eat," and then thanked GOD that he had been allowed to suffer for Him. There are countless representations of him. His most familiar emblem is the gridiron, as in the painting of Gaudentio Ferrari and on English rood-screens, and he is attired as a deacon. In the National Gallery there is a painting of S. Laurence, who bears a palm and crucifix. Sometimes he has a bag in his hand and is distributing money to the poor, as in the painting of Fra Angelico, who also painted scenes from his life which are in the Vatican. In the Church of S. Laurence at Norwich we see him extended on the gridiron.

S. Clement I, Pope and Martyr, the companion of S. Paul, often appears in art. Legend tells that he was banished to the marble quarries of Cherson in the Crimea, and there drowned in the sea with an anchor tied to his neck, by order of the Emperor Trajan. He appears on many English rood-screens and ancient frescoes. His usual symbol is an anchor in his hand or at his feet, and he wears a mitre or tiara and bears a triple crown. Callot represents him floating, with an anchor tied to his neck.

## CHAPTER VI

### *Animals as Symbols*

ANIMAL forms are frequently used as symbols of saints. We have already alluded to the lion of S. Mark. It also appears as the symbol of S. Jerome, with whom it is constantly associated. He was the most learned of the Latin Fathers, the translator of the Bible into the Latin tongue, the pupil of S. Gregory Nazianzen, and secretary of Pope Damarus. His connection with the lion is founded on the well-known story of his extracting a thorn from a lion's foot, as depicted by Antonio da Fiore, Cosimo Roselli, and other artists. The grateful beast is by his side in the paintings of Pietro Perugino, Domenichino, Filippino Lippi, and others.

In our English rood-screens the lion is at his feet, and his other emblems are an ink-horn, scroll, cross, and staff. In allusion to his self-mortification, Raphael and others painted him with a stone in his hand, or beating his breast with a stone, or kneeling on thorns, or wearing a garment woven with thorns. Legend states that, being elated by his eloquence and by his skill in writing, he saw a vision, and was reproved by the words which he beheld, *Ciceronianus es.* This story forms the subject of a picture by Domenichino.

Other saints are associated with the lion. S. Prisca, whose name remains among the black-letter saints of the English Church Calendar, who died for the Faith at the early age of thirteen years in 268 A.D., during the Diocletian persecution, has this animal for her symbol. This is in allusion to the story of her martyrdom. After being beaten with rods she was thrown to the wild beasts; but a lion crouched like a lamb at her feet, and drove away all who would harm her. She was ultimately beheaded. Her other emblems are an eagle, defending her remains from other beasts of prey, and a sword, the instrument of her martyrdom.

S. Theckla, the devoted disciple of S. Paul, has, among many other symbols, the head of a lion at her feet ; and also S. Adrian, captain of the guards of the Emperor Galerius, and his brave wife S. Natalia, who were martyred A.D. 300, have the same emblem.

S. Gerasimus, a fifth-century hermit, has a lion carrying a bucket of water. He acquired great power over animals. His ass fetched water from a distance for him every day. He healed a lion whose eye had been injured by a splinter of wood, and made him lead the ass to pasture and to fetch water. One day the ass was stolen, and the lion, being suspected of having devoured it, was condemned to carry water in its stead. Hence the symbol.

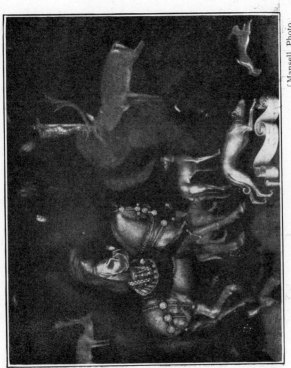

Plate 17.

[Mansell, Photo.

VISION OF S. EUSTACE. (See pages 73 and 74.)

*Plate* 18.

Rubens]                                        [Brogi, Photo.

S. IGNATIUS.   (See page 73.)

S. Ignatius, slain by lions in the amphitheatre at Rome, by order of the Emperor
Trajan, in 107 A.D., has that animal for his
emblem. As they tore his body the name
JESUS was discovered engraven on his heart.
Legend tells that he was the little child
whom JESUS took in His arms when He
said, "Of such is the kingdom of heaven";
and the celestial strains of angelic harps
sounded in his ears and taught him the
music of heaven. Besides the lion, the
sacred monogram and the harp are his
symbols. The king of beasts dug the
grave of S. Mary of Egypt, whose strange
story we have no space to tell, and caused
the martyrdom of SS. Silvanus and
Agapetus.

The stag often appears in Christian
Art. Following the teaching of the verse
in the Psalms, "Like as the hart desireth
the water-brooks," it is taken to signify
holy aspirations, or an emblem of solitude
and purity of life. It is the symbol of
SS. Hubert and Eustache or Eustace.

They both saw a stag with a cross between its antlers. Hubert is distinguished from Eustace by being dressed as a huntsman with his horn, or by wearing episcopal robes, while the latter is attired as a Roman soldier. He was Bishop of Maestricht in the eighth century. Eustache was the master of the horse of the Emperor Trajan, and was originally known as Placidus. The stag he saw spake to him, "O Placidus, why do you pursue me? I am Christ, Whom you ignorantly worship; your alms have ascended to Me, and for this reason I am come to you." We need not follow his adventurous life or witness his martyrdom, with that of his wife and two sons, who were roasted to death inside a brazen bull.

S. Aidan, Bishop of Lindisfarne, has for his emblem a stag crouching at his feet, and also a lighted torch, symbol of the light of truth which he shed on the northern regions of England. He gave to a priest journeying by sea a phial of oil, which calmed a storm and saved the lives of those in the ship, and by his prayer extinguished the flames that Penda had lighted at Bamborough. These incidents are represented in pictures of the saint.

The cow is shown as the attribute of SS. Perpetua and Felicitas, who were tossed by this animal in the amphitheatre when they were martyred. The former has also the attribute of a ladder, which she saw in a vision, guarded by a dragon and set with sharp knives and cruel hooks. A unicorn is the emblem of S. Justina of Antioch, though it has also by an error been conferred on her namesake of Padua, who perished in the persecution of Nero.

The horse, bear, ass, dog, and pig appear as attributes of saints. A pig is the emblem of S. Anthony, the hermit, whose story is well known. He was tempted by demons in the form of lions, bears, leopards, bulls, scorpions, and wolves, and lived in a deserted fort across the Nile, the abode of reptiles, which fled at his approach. Some accounts state that he was originally a swineherd, hence his emblem ; but he was the son of rich and noble parents, and when he relinquished his wealth he possibly fed pigs. This symbol is shown in Pisano's picture in the National Gallery, and in Westminster Abbey he appears as a bearded figure in frock and scapular, with a pig at his side. Sometimes he has a goat with him, a symbol of evil, as Satan, disguised in that form, is said to have tempted him.

Let us glance at the symbol of another S. Anthony—S. Anthony of Padua—born at Lisbon in 1195, who entered the Order of S. Francis, travelling far, preaching the Word in many lands. Like S. Francis, he loved animals, and at Rimini preached to the fishes, some of which are said to have emitted sounds, others opened their mouths, and all inclined their heads. Many artists have loved to depict the saint, and to record this incident. Velas-

quez painted him holding a net over a
bowl of water, and a boy standing by with
fish on a plate.  Murillo shows him with
a book in his left hand, a crucifix in his
right, and the holy Infant Jesus standing
near ; and in another picture represents
him kneeling, with a bowl and a cross.
Raphael gives him a lily as his emblem,
and in the chapel of the Eremitani at
Padua he is shown with a lily and a book.
At Padua there is a bas-relief showing an
ass kneeling to the saint, who is holding
the Blessed Sacrament.  Several Italian
painters represent him dressed in the
Franciscan habit without any symbol.  In
the Vatican he is depicted with a flame of
fire in his hand ; Pesillino shows him
finding a miser's heart in a money-chest ;
and Garofalo, in his painting of S. Cecilia
playing on an organ, shows the Virgin and
S. Anthony listening to her.

A white dove is the symbol of S. Polycarp, the dove that rose from the ashes of
the saintly Bishop of Smyrna after his

martyrdom, and soared heavenwards, the odour of frankincense having come from the saint's body, and his blood having quenched the flames.

## CHAPTER VII

### *Some English Saints*

NOT without some noble representatives of the English nation is the catalogue of saints complete, and many bright examples of living faith and patient witnessing for CHRIST have shone forth in our island. Foremost amongst these stands S. Alban, the protomartyr of Britain, whose memory is preserved by the stately Abbey Church, now the Cathedral of St. Albans. His life-story is too well known to be here chronicled, how he rescued and sheltered S. Amphibalus and was converted by him to the Faith. On refusing to sacrifice to the pagan deities he was ordered to be scourged and then beheaded. On his way to execution the crowd throng-

ing the bridge S. Alban dried up the river
Ver, and in order to assuage his thirst a
fountain sprang up near him. Bede states
that the executioner was suddenly converted to Christianity and craved to die
with him. Some legends state that the
eyes of the executioner dropped out of
their sockets when he was ordered to slay
the saint, whose fate he shared. This is
shown in an illuminated manuscript of
Matthew of Paris, at the British Museum,
in a painting at St. Albans Abbey, and on
the seal of Binham Priory. In the brass
of Abbot Delamere at the Abbey there is
a representation of the saint with a tall
cross, a clerical cap, and a sword. This
last, the instrument of his martyrdom, is
his usual emblem, sometimes with a palm
and crucifix, as at the Church of S. Mary,
Schnurgrasse, Cologne. In the Beau-
champ Chapel at Warwick there is a glass
window containing a figure of the saint in
armour, wearing a robe and coronet with
a sceptre and Calvary cross. He is also

depicted spreading his cloak, the sun
shining upon him. His best memorial is
the beautiful Abbey Church, originally
founded by King Offa, in A.D. 793, near
the scene of his martyrdom.

S. Aldhelm, Bishop and Confessor,
second Abbot of Malmesbury and first
Bishop of Sherborne, was the light of the
Church of England at the end of the seventh
century. Learned in Greek and Hebrew,
he bestowed lustre on the Church by his
attainments. He was the foremost church-
builder of his age. The little church at
Bradford-on-Avon still stands as his
memorial. Music also owned him as a
gentle promoter. There is a bronze
figure of the saint on the Digby monument in the church at Sherborne. He
is represented in episcopal dress playing
on a harp.

S. Frideswide, the patron saint of
Oxford Cathedral, formerly the Priory of
S. Frideswide, lived in the eighth century.
Her father Didan built a convent for her,

but Algar, Prince of Mercia, wished to marry her, and swore that he would carry her off. She fled for refuge. When she returned to Oxford she was gallantly defended by the men of the town against Algar, who was struck blind, but his sight was restored at the prayer of the saint. Incidents in her life are represented in the beautiful stained glass window in the Latin Chapel of the Cathedral, designed by Sir Edward Burne-Jones. Her attributes are a crown and sceptre of curious pattern with heavy foliage, and sometimes she has an ox by her side.

Some carved bosses and corbels in Lichfield Cathedral record the life of S. Chad, first bishop of that see. He is represented in episcopal robes with his pastoral staff.

S. Richard of Chichester in early life worked on his brother's farm as a labourer. Callot depicts him ploughing. He lived during the stormy reign of Henry III, when the revenues of his see were pur-

loined by the king's ministers. A chalice
is his emblem, sometimes placed at his
feet, or before the kneeling saint.

Ecclesiastical history tells no sweeter
story than that of the life of the saintly
Anselm. It has been often told from the
time of the Saxon Eadmer to that of
Dean Church. He is represented in art
with the Blessed Virgin and the Infant
Jesus appearing to him, sometimes holding the model of a ship, and Callot
depicts him exorcising an evil spirit from
a monk.

S. Dunstan was the most powerful and
conspicuous character in the Church and
State of England in the tenth century.
Whether as monk of Glastonbury or
primate he fearlessly did his duty and
left an imperishable memory. Many
legends cluster around his name. There
is a figure of him in the Bodleian Library
at Oxford, representing the saint seizing
the devil with pincers. Once his harp
hanging on a wall poured forth celestial

melody.   A harp is his symbol, and in one picture a dove is whispering at his ear.

S. Wilfrid is represented baptizing pagans.

S. Edward the Confessor is shown on several English rood-screens holding a sceptre and a ring, and sometimes a purse hangs from his right arm.

S. John of Beverley has his shrine at his side.

The Venerable Bede holds a pitcher with lights from heaven shining upon him.

S. Hugh of Lincoln has many symbols. Van Assen in his painting in the Munich Gallery shows him with a swan at his feet. Callot represents his dream of the seven stars, which also appears in the sculpture of S. Mary's spire, Oxford.   A mitre, three flowers in his hand, a lantern, an angel protecting him from lightning, are his other emblems.

S. Edmund, King of the East Saxons, who was captured by the Danes, bound to a tree and shot with arrows, has for his symbol an arrow, which he bears in his hand or offers to heaven. It is sometimes conjoined with a sceptre or a globe. On the Colney font he is shown bound to a tree and shot with arrows. Callot represents a wolf guarding his body, and Burgmaier painted a bear seated before him.

S. Thomas of Canterbury, the martyred prelate, is depicted in countless mural paintings and other works of art. On our English rood-screens he usually appears with a crozier which has a battle-axe head, and he bears an archiepiscopal cross, or a sword in his hand or in his head, or he wears a mitre. Burgmaier represents him wearing his pallium and washing the feet of a leper.

S. Wulstan, of Worcester, was the last of the English bishops who retained his see under the rule of William the Conqueror. Legend tells of the endeavour of the Norman prelates to deprive him of

*Plate* 19.

Duez]

S. CUTHBERT. (See page 87.)

his bishopric, and how the marble tomb of the Confessor refused to yield back the episcopal staff to any other hand than his. One of the bishops holding the head of the monument of King John in his cathedral is believed to represent S. Wulstan and the other S. Oswald.

S. Cuthbert, of Lindisfarne, who died A.D. 687, saw angels bearing the soul of S. Aidan to heaven. With him is connected the legend of the Dun Cow, and the remains of his shrine, his coffin, robes, maniple, and pastoral cross may still be seen at Durham.

S. Alphege, Archbishop of Canterbury, was martyred by the Danes in 1012.

S. Boniface, the Apostle of the Germans, martyred by the Frisians in 755, an Englishman, has many emblems. On the coins of the Abbey of Fulda he appears with a book pierced by a sword. In the church at Munich he is shown felling Thor's oak, and in an old engraving an axe is laid at the root of the oak, and an angel is bringing to the saint a fish. A hand giving to him a cross, a scourge, the saint beaten to death with a club, a sword upon a book, and the saint striking the ground with his archiepiscopal cross, causing water to spring up, are some of the symbols of the brave S. Boniface.

S. Columba's life needs no description. His famous monastery of Iona was the centre of light in the northern land, and from it shone forth a radiance which converted northern England to CHRIST. S. Columba was kind and loving to all, and, like S. Francis, he was devoted to birds and beasts. He subdued the fierceness of the wild beasts, and the no less wild tribes of Scotland ; hence he is represented in the *Icones Sanctorum* as taming a wild beast, and kneeling among wolves. We see the saint in a bear's den with a fountain near him, the well of life, from which he drank freely himself, and watered the thirsty hearts of the nations. Sunbeams shining over his head tell of the light shed upon him which he reflected on all who came beneath the influence of this holy man. The life of S. Columba, written by S. Adamnan, Abbot of Iona in A.D. 679, and translated by Wentworth Huyshe, has just been published. It is one of the earliest complete literary compositions written in the British Isles. The emblem of the sunbeams shining over the saint's head is explained by the following incident: "Cruithnechan the priest, foster-father of the blessed boy, found his house irradiated by bright light —for he saw a globe of fire stationary over the face of the little sleeping boy. And seeing it he understood that the grace of the HOLY SPIRIT was poured out from heaven upon his foster-child."

S. Osmund, Bishop of Salisbury (A.D. 1099), is represented with the book of the Sarum Use in his hand.

The catalogue of English saints is by no means exhausted, but space will not permit of a further enumeration. Many of them also lack symbols, as the English artists were not so prolific as the Italian and other foreign old masters, who sought for subjects in the Hagiography of their own country.

## CHAPTER VIII

### *Some Popes*

MANY of the occupants of the Papal throne in times of severe persecution have laid down their lives for their faith and have attained to saintship. Many have been canonized for their virtues and pious lives, and foremost amongst them stands S. Gregory the Great. His life is the history of the Church in the sixth century. The art of music owes to him the school of plainsong, the Gregorian chant which bears his name. He abridged the Gelasian Office of the Mass. His sage advice to Augustine, the Apostle of the English, is well known—not to insist upon a rigid uniformity, but counselling the use of all pious and good customs suitable for new times and new countries. His censure of Serenus, Bishop of Marseilles, for pulling down some hangings adorned with sacred subjects on the grounds that the people worshipped them is appropriately recorded here :

" Antiquity hath not without reason admitted the paintings of the lives of the saints in sacred buildings. In that you forbade them to be adored, we entirely applaud you ; but in that you broke them, we blame you—for a picture supplies to ignorant people who gaze at it what Scripture doth to them that read."

S. Gregory often appears in art. He may be seen in the Church of S. John the Evangelist at Parma, in company with S. Mark, and the Dove, signifying the HOLY SPIRIT, whispering into his ear. A large iron ring round his body is another emblem of the saint. John the Deacon, who wrote his life, states :

" His picture was long extant, representing him as of moderate stature, with dark hair in two thin waving curls on the forehead, a large tonsure, dark yellow beard, ruddy complexion (it latterly got jaundiced), and thick parted lips, with a chestnut-coloured chasuble and dalmatic on, and the pallium twisted round his shoulders." His belt of white byssus, (unpierced by needles), his relic-case, made of thin silver, which he wore round his neck, and the belt only a thumb's breadth wide, were customarily kissed on the vigil of his anniversary in the ninth century.

Another Pope, S. Leo the Great, must not be omitted. He lived when Attila, King of the Huns, the Scourge of GOD, attacked Rome, and his majestic appearance, together with the miraculous apparition of SS. Peter and Paul, saved the city from the barbarians. Raphael and the sculptor Algardi have told the story, and the saint appears with the two Apostles in the painting by Callot. Sometimes he appears on horseback, Attila and his sol-

diers kneeling before him, or praying at
the tomb of S. Peter.  He died in A.D. 461.

Many other Popes have been martyred
and canonized.  S. Anicetus, the friend
and contemporary of S. Polycarp, suffered
death in A.D. 153, being broken on a
wheel, which became his symbol.  S. Cletus,
the successor of Linus, was martyred in
A.D. 91, and Marcellinus in 298.  S. Pius,
Pope and Martyr, met his death under the
rule of Antonius Pius in A.D. 157.  The
Hermas who wrote *The Shepherd* is said
to have been his brother.  The Sarum
Martyrology styles him S. Pituouse, and
states that he " ordeyned eester day to be
kepte always upon the Sondays."  His
symbol is an oval with the sacred monogram.  S. Stephen, Pope, was martyred
in A.D. 257.  During that time of severe
persecutions he sought refuge in the Catacombs, where he was killed, by order of
the Emperor, while he was celebrating the
Holy Eucharist.  His body rested for many
centuries in the Catacombs of S. Calixtus,

but was subsequently removed to Pisa. A sword in his breast is his emblem, and he is also represented stabbed in his back at the altar.

S. Sylvester was Pope of Rome when Constantine the Great was converted to Christianity. Tradition states that the Emperor, who suffered from leprosy, saw in a vision the Apostles SS. Peter and Paul, who advised him to be baptized by Sylvester, and said if he obeyed his disease would depart. The Pope had been compelled to seek safety in a secret retreat on Mount Soracte. He was discovered, and consented to baptize the Emperor, whose leprosy at once disappeared. But tradition errs. Constantine was not baptized until the end of his life, and Eusebius performed the ceremony. Sylvester ruled the Church well. A tiara, double cross, and a scroll are his emblems. Sometimes he appears bearing a cross and an olive-branch. An ox lying by his side is one of his symbols. Callot represents him baptizing Constantine, and in another picture a female is shown bearing to him a label, " *Silvester sc me tua salva pce.*"

Amongst the martyred Popes of the third century we may mention S. Zephyrinus, whose symbol is a monstrance, and S. Calixtus, after whom the catacomb is named. He was drowned, and his symbol is a millstone. S. Fabianus, another martyred Pope, has for his emblems a dove and a sword, Cornelius a horn (probably a play upon his name), and S. Sixtus II, slain in the catacombs, bears for his emblem a sword.

## CHAPTER IX

### *The Founders of the Religious Orders*

AMONG those who have been deemed worthy of canonization are the founders of the great Religious Orders. Foremost among them stands the holy Benedict (A.D. 480–543), the founder of the Benedictine Order of monks. On Mount Cassino, where stood a temple of Apollo, he constructed his monastery. Some monks who liked not his strict rule tried in vain to poison him. When he made the sign of the cross over the poisoned cup, it broke into fragments. One of his emblems is a sieve. In his young days his nurse, who followed him to his lonely retreat in the desert, broke a sieve, which the saint mended by his prayers. A raven was his companion, and shared his meals. Florentius, a monk envious of the reputation of S. Benedict, tried to kill him with a poisoned loaf. He ordered the bird to convey it to a place where it would do no harm. Countless stories are told of his sanctity and the wonders that he worked. In art he is usually represented in the habit of his order, which was originally white, but afterwards changed to black, and his symbols are a raven and a broken sieve.

Few have left so great an impress on his age as the famous founder of the Cistercian Order, S. Bernard, Abbot of Clairvaux. His home was at Fontaines, near Dijon. He owed much to the influence of a pious mother, and was a gentle, thoughtful, studious, and silent boy. He resolved to devote himself to the monastic life, and induced his brothers to join him. They, with their father and their companions, were admitted to the monastery of Citeaux, which became too

*Plate* 20.

S. BENEDICT.
(See page 97.)

strait for the numbers who wished to join
the Cistercian Order. Other foundations
were made, and in the Valley of Worm-
wood, a nest of robbers, Bernard was
permitted to raise his famous House of
Clairvaux, or "Bright Valley." There
the community endured at first great
poverty. Porridge made of beech-leaves
was their diet—a food that had no savour
but what was given to it by hunger or by
the love of GOD. Bernard spent his days
in toil, in severe study, and the most
rigorous mortifications. The glory of
more than mortal purity seemed to sur-
round him, and miracles attended his
progress. Dignities were offered to him,
but he declined to accept them. He
espoused the cause of Pope Innocent at
the time of the great schism. Of the
events of his wondrous life, his contest
with Abelard, his preaching the second
crusade, his vigorous writings and con-
demnation of abuses it is unnecessary to
write here. The life of the saint is known

*Plate* 21.

Perugino]　　　　　　　　　　　　　　[Brogi, Photo.

S. BERNARD AND S. JOHN OF THE CROSS.

(See pages 98 and 100–3.)

to the world—that life that ended at his
monastery at Clairvaux, where he ascended
"from the 'Bright Valley' to the mountain
of eternal brightness."

Many emblems have artists given to the
saint.  On account of the severity of his
mortifications, the *Arbor Pastoralis* shows
him bearing the instruments of our
Saviour's Passion.  The Blessed Virgin
with the Infant Saviour are represented
as appearing to him, and in two pictures
she gives him milk from her breast.
Garofalo painted him with three mitres
on his book or at his feet—those mitres
which he rejected.  In the Dresden Gallery there is a picture of him with a beehive as his symbol, in allusion to his
honeyed words, and sometimes an angel
holds his crozier while he writes his burning words.  A white dog, which sometimes has a red back, is also his emblem,
and in the Isabella Breviary at the British
Museum he is shown holding the devil in
a chain.  Such are some emblems which

artists have loved to assign to the brave, lionhearted, holy S. Bernard.

S. Bruno, Confessor (R.K.), A.D. 1101, the founder of the Carthusian Order, was born at Cologne, and was regarded as the light of the Churches, the doctor of doctors, the glory of Germany and France, the ornament of the age, the model of good men, and the mirror of the world. Rheims was the scene of his earlier labours. In 1084 he went with six companions to Grenoble, and soon established his monastery at Chartreuse, a dismal solitude beset with high rocks, covered with snow and fogs. The rule was very strict. After some years he was called to Rome by Urban II, in order to advise the Pope on weighty matters. A court and palace pleased not the saint, and after some time he was permitted to retire to Calabria, where he founded a second monastery, that of De la Torre. He wrote many works ; his commentaries on the Psalms and Epistles of S. Paul show him to have been one of the most learned men of his age. A crucifix is his usual emblem, which sometimes has leaves and flowers at the ends ; or it rests on a palm-branch. A star on his breast and a globe beneath his feet are other symbols of the holy S. Bruno.

S. Francis of Assisi, the holy founder of the Franciscan Order, needs no biography. His life is known and read of all men. Artists have lavished their highest skill on representations of him. Giotto's painting in the Louvre of the sermon to the birds represents the saint's love for animals. Birds suffered him to touch them, and they even would not depart from him. When he preached, swallows ceased their twittering, and at his word were still. Two years before his death, when he was fasting at Laverna, an angel, bearing the image of the Crucified, appeared to him, and impressed the marks of the nails and spear on his hands and feet and side. This act of receiving the sacred stigmata is chronicled

Plate **22.**

Giotto]

[Anderson, Photo.

S. FRANCIS OF ASSISI. (See page 104.)

in many works of art. He is often depicted wearing the crown of thorns and carrying a cross. A lily is sometimes his emblem, and also a lamb, as in Giotto's painting. Scenes from his life are depicted in the church at Assisi. Ghirlandajo painted roses springing from his blood, and another picture shows him ascending to heaven in a fiery chariot.

The life of S. Dominic, the founder of the Order of Preaching Friars, styled also Dominicans, or, from the colour of their habits, Black Friars, has been often told. He was a Spaniard of noble birth, and became an Augustinian canon. He accompanied the Bishop of Osma and some Cistercian Abbots on a mission to the Albigenses. He preached to the heretics with fiery enthusiasm ; and, though he was ever more ready to suffer martyrdom than to inflict it, he took some part in that terrible crusade against the Albigenses. One day he saw a vision : the Blessed Virgin was interceding with the Saviour, Who was

*Plate* 23.

Fra Angelico]       [Brogi, Photo.

S. DOMINIC.

(See page 106.)

about to destroy the world for its iniquities, and she was presenting to Him S. Dominic and S. Francis, with a promise that they would convert the world. S. Dominic founded his Order at Toulouse in A.D. 1216. The zeal and fervour of his preaching, his enthusiasm for the conversion of souls, his love of poverty, left their mark upon the world and survived in his followers. There is a fine picture of the saint in the National Gallery, by Mario Zoppo, showing him preaching with a book and rosary in his left hand. His usual emblem is a lily, as in the pictures of Fra Angelico, Alexis Baldovinetti, D. Fabi (Vienna Gallery), and of other artists. Sometimes he has a star over his head, or on his forehead or his breast. A book, a cross, and rosary are also his symbols. A dog firing a globe also appears in several representations of the saint. Angelico de Fiesole depicts him curing a wounded youth, the nephew of Cardinal Stephen of Fossa Nuova. A fresco at Rome shows him receiving the keys from S. Peter, and Niccolo Pisano depicts him receiving the commission to preach from SS. Peter and Paul. As a representation of the sterner side of his nature, Angelico represents him holding a sword, while books are burning at his side. Few saints have been more frequently represented in art than S. Dominic.

The founder of the Order of Bonhommes, S. Francis of Paula, died in 1508. Only two houses of this Order existed in England, Ashridge and Eddington. He had the word " *caritas* " ever on his lips, and hated detraction. Hence that word, appearing in rays of light, is his emblem. In the Louvre there is a painting of him standing on his cloak on the sea, and he also appears with his staff, a crucifix, and rosary.

S. Ignatius, the founder and first general of the Order of Jesuits, has left his mark upon history. He wrote *Constitutiones Societatis Jesu*, and this work, with his hand resting upon it, and the sacred monogram above in light, appear as his symbols in the painting by Rubens at Warwick Castle. The sacred monogram on his breast, or within rays in his hand, is his constant emblem.

S. Francis de Sales, Bishop of Geneva, who died in 1622, founded the Order of the Nuns of the Visitation of the Blessed Virgin. He admired architecture, painting, music, and nature, and deemed them mystic ladders for mounting heavenwards. He is often represented in art holding his heart in his hand.

The Spanish saint, S. Peter Nolasco, who died in 1256, founded the Order of the Redemption of Christian captives among the Moors.

Another founder of an Order was S. Norbert, Bishop and Confessor, A.D. 1134. He was a wild and gay youth at the court of the Emperor Henry V, of noble family and rich possessions, and was continuing in his evil courses when GOD called him,

as He did Saul of Tarsus, by a lightning-
flash, and changed his life. He craved
ordination from the Bishop of Cologne,
had much trouble with the lax canons of
the cathedral, whose ways he tried to re-
form, and then established the Order of
the Praemonstratensians, or White Canons,
in the wild region of Prémontré, and
later on was appointed Archbishop of
Magdeburg in Prussia. In the Vatican
there is a painting of S. Norbert by
Fil. Bigioli, representing him holding
up a chalice with the Sacred Host in
his right hand. He is depicted carrying
a monstrance with the Blessed Sacrament, sometimes with an angel holding
a monstrance before him. According
to one legend, recorded by Callot, his
episcopal vestments were brought to him
by the Blessed Virgin. In the *Ikonographie*
his emblem is a chalice with a spider in it,
alluding to the legend that one day, when
he was celebrating mass, a poisonous
spider fell into the hallowed chalice, but

unhesitatingly he drank the contents, and miraculously his life was spared. The devil, chained or at his feet, appears in some figures, and an attempted assassination of the saint in a confessional is recorded by Gueffier. S. Norbert has lacked no limner to record his saintly life.

Plate 24.

S. GREGORY THE GREAT.　(See pages 92 and 115.)　　I

Plate 25.

S. AUGUSTINE. (See pages 116 and 133.)

# CHAPTER X

## *Doctors*

THE four great Doctors of the Church are S. Gregory, S. Jerome, S. Ambrose, and S. Augustine. We have already recorded the symbols and chief events in the lives of the two first, S. Gregory and S. Jerome. We will now allude to the other learned and devoted followers of CHRIST.

S. Ambrose was Archbishop of Milan, and the honour due unto this noble and saintly man is shown in all the Churches. He it was who daringly withstood the great Emperor Theodosius, whose hands were red with the blood of the slaughtered people of Thessalonica. S. Ambrose imposed a fitting penance, and eight months passed before the emperor was received again into the company of the faithful. He was a comforter of S. Monica during her sorrow on account of the errors of her son, and at last was able to baptize the repentant Augustine. The grandest of our Christian hymns, *Te Deum laudamus*, is by some attributed to him. His emblem is a scourge and a cross ; a tower and a beehive are also his principal symbols.

S. Augustine, the saintly Bishop of Hippo, was the light of the Church in the early part of the fifth century. A perfect model of true penitence, a true champion of the Faith, a confounder of heresies, a prolific and spiritual writer, S. Augustine has left a name revered throughout Christendom. Of his early sins and heretical tendencies, so graphically described in his *Confessions*, of his struggles with the heretical Donatists, Manichees, Arians, and Pelagians it is unnecessary here to write. His praises have been sung by the learned of every age. Luther affirmed that since the Apostles' time the

Church never had a better doctor. He
has been styled the " bright star of philo-
sophy," the singular, excellent father, and
the chief among the greatest ornaments
and lights of the Church. In Augustinian
monasteries pictures of the saint are frequent. Old paintings too show him clad
in a black habit with a leathern girdle.
An inflamed heart is a constant symbol of
the saint, and this frequently appears with
an arrow, as in the painting by Meister
von Liesborn in the National Gallery. In
the same collection there is a painting by
Garafalo of S. Augustine with a child and
a spoon on the sea-shore, and Murillo's
painting at the Louvre and a primer of
1516 represent the same event. A light
from heaven shining upon him with the
word " *Veritas*," and an eagle, are some
other symbols of the saint.

Other doctors of the Church are
S. Thomas of Aquin, or Thomas Aquinas,
the " Angelic Doctor," the " Eagle of
Divines," " Angel of the Schools," the

Universal Doctor, whose emblem is a silver net knit with precious stones of various hues, implying the purity of his life and the harmony of his doctrines.

S. Peter Martyr was murdered in 1252. He was a Dominican of Verona, and was styled *Virgo, doctor et martyr, corona triplici laureatus,* and was canonized by Innocent IV. In 1340 his body was translated to the Church of S. Eustorgius at Milan, where it rests in a fine tomb. Titian and Guido and other artists have displayed their genius on the subject of Peter Martyr's death. Titian's famous picture was burnt in the Church of SS. John and Paul at Venice in 1867. Guido's picture is in the Gallery at Bologna. The martyr is shown in the painting at the Church of S. Dominic, Orvieto, as falling by the sword with three crowns over his head. Crivelli represents him with a knife in his hand. In the Pitti Gallery, Fra Angelico shows him with a cut across his head and a palm in his hand. A sixteenth-century

*Plate* 26.

S. THOMAS AQUINAS.
(See page 117.)

painting represents him with a knife in his hand and a sword in his heart. Guercino's painting in the Milan Gallery shows him kneeling, with a sabre at his feet, and the same artist has a painting in the National Gallery of the saint being martyred in a wood, with angels appearing. An old print shows him writing "*Credo*" on the ground with his blood at his martyrdom.

S. Athanasius, Bishop of Alexandria, the story of whose life is the history of the Church in the fourth century, who gallantly contended for the Faith against Arianism, is represented in art as a Greek archbishop with the pallium, standing between two columns, and is sometimes depicted with heretics beneath his feet.

# CHAPTER XI

## *Hermits*

AMONGST holy hermits we must record S. Paul, the first of the Anchorites (A.D. 342). When the Decian Persecution raged, Paul, a rich young Egyptian Christian, fled into the country, and afterwards sought a safer resting-place in mountain solitudes in a cave. A palm-tree grew beside the entrance, and gave him food and clothing. Wild beasts prowled around. Ravens brought him bread. Hither came S. Anthony to visit the aged hermit, and anon buried him in the cloak which Athanasius had given him. A vision revealed to him the happy end of the holy man, who was borne upwards by hosts of angels to Paradise. His symbols are his dress of palm-leaves and the ravens which fed him.

S. Giles, another hermit (A.D. 700), has been held in great veneration in France and England, and many churches are dedicated to him, usually those situated on the outskirts of a town, in allusion to the solitary life of the saint.   He was a native of Athens, and, wandering to France, fixed his hermitage in the open deserts of Nisnes. He lived on wild roots and herbs and the milk of a hind in the forest.   One day a prince was hunting, and the hind fled to the saint for protection.   The King of France greatly esteemed the holy hermit, and gave him land for a monastery, which grew up at that place into a very large and flourishing abbey.   In the English rood-screens he is usually shown with a hind lying at his feet, or resting her foot on his knee, the other foot being wounded with an arrow.   The font at Warwick Church shows a wounded hind leaping up to him.   Albert Durer's representation of

*Plate* 27.

S. ANTHONY.

(See pages 75 and 121.)

*Plate* 28.

S. GILES.
(See page 122.)

S. Giles, now at the British Museum, shows him standing with a book in his right hand, his left hand wounded with an arrow, in the act of protecting a hind leaping up to him. Molanus depicts him imposing his hands over King Charles Martel.

## XII

### *Women Saints and Martyrs*

A GROUP of noble women who laid down their lives for CHRIST's sake stand among the crowd of saints and martyrs. Foremost amongst them is S. Agnes, Roman Virgin and Martyr, the patron saint of virgin purity. Rejecting the offers of marriage, and declaring herself a Christian, she was condemned to stand naked in a public place. Only one base man presumed to gaze at her, and he was struck by lightning. She was finally beheaded. The lamb is her symbol, usually carried in her arms. The pallia sent by the Pope to the archbishops of various provinces were usually made from the wool of two lambs blessed by the Pope on the feast of the saint. Another emblem

*Plate* 29.

S. AGNES.

(See page 126.)

is a dove bearing a ring to this virgin bride of heaven.

The memory of few saints has been revered more highly than that of S. Agatha, a girl of noble birth and of great beauty, who resisted the evil intentions of Quintianus, Praetor of Sicily, and was condemned to torture. She was scourged, had her breasts cut off, and was then thrown into prison. S. Peter and an angel healed her wounds in the night. She was then condemned to be burnt, but an earthquake shook the town, showing the displeasure of heaven. She died in prison, some say after being rolled naked on burning coals and broken glass, which had no power to hurt her. She was buried at Catania, and her veil was placed on her tomb, and was believed to have power against fires and earthquakes. Mediaeval artists have loved to depict her in her trials and sufferings. Her usual emblem is a pair of pincers, and other symbols are a veil, a plate, on which rest those lacerated parts of her tender body, and a chafing-dish, in allusion to her fiery ordeal. There are mosaic portraits of the saint at Ravenna and in the Church of S. Cecilia, Trastevere, of the ninth century. In the National Gallery there is a painting of her martyrdom by Sebastiano del Piombo, and Vandyck, Domenichino, and others have depicted scenes from her life. She is the guardian saint of nursing mothers, and the helper of all who suffer from the breast.

S. Dorothy, Virgin and Martyr, was beheaded at Caesarea in Cappadocia in the early years of the fourth century. When condemned by Apricius as a witch, she said, "I will suffer anything for CHRIST, my LORD and Spouse, in Whose garden of delight I shall gather roses and apples, and be glad with Him for ever." Theophilus, the scribe, asked her scornfully to send him some of the roses. Just before her execution a strange unearthly child brought to her some roses ; she begged the child to take them to Theophilus, who

was converted by this means, and soon
followed her from earth by the thorny
road of martyrdom.   Her figure appears
in the Chapel of Henry VII at Westminster.   The rose which she sent by the
heavenly messenger is her usual emblem,
and also apples.   Every year, on her feast
day (February 6th), roses and apples
are blessed at Rome in memory of the
legend.

S. Apollonia, Virgin and Martyr of
Alexandria, has for her symbol a pair of
pincers holding a tooth, in allusion to the
cruel tortures which she endured by having
all her teeth drawn before she was burned
to death.   She had been betrayed to the
civil authorities by her father, and, when
called upon to sacrifice to an idol, much
enraged them by casting out the demon
from the image.   Enselius states that
" they beat her cheeks, and knocked out
all the teeth in her head.   Over against
the city they prepared a pile, and threatened
to burn her quick unless she would, to-

Plate 30.

S. APOLLONIA. (See page 130.)

Plate 31.

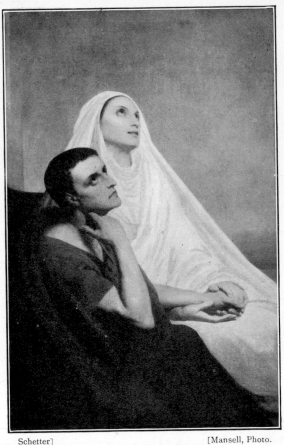

S. AUGUSTINE AND S. MONICA. (See pages 116 and 133.)

gether with them, utter blasphemy. But she, lingering a little while, as though she would take deliberation, suddenly leaped into the fire and was consumed to ashes."

I am following the order in which these names of holy women come in the English or Roman Calendar, and not in chronological order ; so you must be prepared to leap from the records of early Christian martyrs to those of later days. S. Frances, a holy Roman lady, died A.D. 1440. The wife of Lorenzo de Ponzani loved to commune with GOD. Her children, Evangelista and Agnes, were called away from earth. The former appeared to her accompanied by an angel. Her husband released her from her marriage vows, and she entered a convent. She was one of the patron saints of Rome. Her symbol, violets, used to be carried to her tomb, and a public banquet given on her festival. Miguard painted Madame de Maintenon *habillée en Sainte Françoise Romaine*.

S. Monica, the holy mother of S. Augustine, endured many sorrows on account of the errors and youthful follies of her son. You can well remember the pious words of comfort breathed into her ear by S. Ambrose. Pietro Perugino painted her standing behind her son, who is represented kneeling. Sheffer represents them sitting together holding each other's hands, with an enwrapt look upon their faces. Her symbol is a handkerchief, a sign perhaps of the tears she shed, also an open book or a crucifix.

S. Catherine, Virgin and Martyr (A.D. 290) of Alexandria, has been a favourite subject for artists, and her well-known symbol, a wheel, is easily recognized. When only eighteen years of age she was so learned in the liberal arts that she was able to vanquish the sophistries of the philosophers. She was doomed to death, and her murderers wished to torture her by means of a wheel studded with swordpoints, but by her prayers the wheel was broken, though finally she suffered death

Plate 32.

[Brogi, Photo.

Luini]

S. AGNES, S. SCHOLASTICA, S. CATHERINE. (See pages 126 and 134.)

*Plate* 33.

Francesco Vanni]                    [Brogi, Photo.
S. CATHERINE OF SIENA.
(See page 137.)

by the axe. Her usual emblem is the instrument of her martyrdom, a wheel set with spikes. A sword, a palm, and a book are sometimes conjoined with the wheel. Bernardino Luini painted her crowned with white flowers, with the broken wheel and a palm held by an angel. The broken wheel signifies her triumph over the malice of her enemies. Perugino painted her espoused by the Saviour, and in a fresco at Milan she is shown carried by angels to Mount Sinai. Guido, in the Turin Gallery, gives as her emblems a lamb and a palm.

Another S. Catherine lived more than a thousand years later, S. Catherine of Siena (A.D. 1380). Artists have loved to bestow upon this fourteenth-century saint their best skill and highest veneration. She was the daughter of a dyer of Siena, refused to marry, and in order to make herself undesirable in the eyes of young men, cut off her long hair and hid her sweet face behind a veil. Persecuted at first by her parents, she was at length permitted to join the Sisters of the Third Order of S. Dominic, who did not live in nunneries, but worked for their LORD in the world. She was a holy mystic, and had strange visions. The Saviour appeared to her and dispelled the shades of doubt and evil that at one time beset her. There is a painting in the Academy at Florence of the Saviour giving His sacred heart in exchange for her heart, and an angel holding a cross and a crown of thorns. She is often represented as crowned with thorns with a cross or crucifix in her hand. A cross with flowers, a heart with a cross upon it, an inflamed heart, a cross and a book, a crucifix, lily and palm, a flaming heart with the sacred monogram, a dove upon her head, stigmas, a lily and a book, as in the fresco by Razzi in the Church of S. Dominic at Siena—these are some of the symbols of the saint. C. Veronese and Fra Bartolommeo painted her as

*Plate* 34.

Veronese]                    [Mansell, Photo.
S. HELENA.   (See page 140.)

being espoused to the Saviour, both pictures being in the Pitti Gallery at Florence. In the latter the Saviour appears as an infant. Few saints have such a wealth of attributes.

S. Helena, the mother of Constantine the Great, warned by a vision, journeyed to Jerusalem, and there on the site of the Holy Sepulchre discovered the Cross in A.D. 326. She built a noble church called the New Jerusalem for its reception. Half of the Cross she enclosed in a silver chest, and the other half she took to the emperor. She often appears in art bearing or embracing a large cross, and as an empress wearing a crown. Domenichino painted her holding a nail over a chalice, a hammer lying below. As the founder of the church at Jerusalem, she is sometimes represented holding a model of a church in her hand. Caliari's painting of the saint's vision of the Holy Cross borne to her by angels is one of the most beautiful conceptions of S. Helena.

The life of S. Mary Magdalen of Pazzi has been told in Bolland by her confessor, Virgilio Caparis, Soc. Jes., and reveals a wondrous depth of spirituality and Communion with her LORD. From her earliest years she felt the fervour of devotion, and this increased with years. Pazzi was her family name — a noble Florentine house — and Catarina her Christian name, which was abandoned when she became a Carmelite nun, and she was henceforth known as Sister Maria Maddalena. Many stories are told of her piety and devotion. She loved to study the *Soliloquies* of S. Augustine, hence she is represented in the *Die Attribute* with that saint appearing to her and inscribing on her heart the words *Verbum caro factum est*. In other artistic representations she appears receiving the Blessed Sacrament from our Saviour or a white veil from the Blessed Virgin. A crown of thorns is another symbol of the saint, alluding to her early desire to suffer something for our LORD, which caused her to wear a crown of prickly orange-sprays, binding it so tightly about her head that she could not sleep. An inflamed heart and a crown of thorns are given as her symbols in the *Ikonographie*, and in an engraving we see her crowned with thorns, embracing a cross, while rays dart on her from a monstrance. Luca Giordana represents her as being presented to the Saviour by an angel.

S. Margaret, queen and widow (A.D. 1093), is the patron saint of Scotland. It was a storm, friendly to the northern land, that bore her and her brother Edgar Atheling thither. Malcolm Canmore married the saintly princess, who was a rare impersonation of feminine grace, and a true memorial of the highest Christian sanctity. All that is best in womanhood found a living expression in her life. Her court was pure ; her husband a devoted king through her influence, and the Church reformed by her zeal. Her almsgiving was universal. She served CHRIST daily with food in the person of 300 poor people. Personal austerity marked her life, and when her husband was slain in battle, and her son tried to keep back from her the fatal news, she appealed to him by the black rood which she was clasping in her hands, to tell her the truth, and even thanked GOD that He had sent her pain even at the last. That black rood is the emblem of the saintly Margaret. In Bonn Cathedral she is represented holding it, and in Callot's portrait, which also shows her visiting the sick. A sceptre and book are the symbols assigned to her on the seal of the Prior of Pluscardine. The Church and Monastery of Dumfermline were founded by her.

S. Juliana Falconieri (A.D. 1340) was the daughter of one of the seven noble Florentines who abandoned the world for contemplation and prayer, and were known as "The servants of Mary." They retired for solitude to Monte Sanario, not far from the city of Florence, and the faithful saint built the beautiful church of Annunziata. In the church is a series of paintings of the life and miracles of S. Fillippo Benizzi, the head of the Order of "The servants of Mary," who assigned to her care the Brethren and Sisters of the Order. In the Florence Academy there is a painting of S. Juliana with the Sacred Host on her heart, and she is also represented in an old engraving as praying before the Blessed Sacrament.

S. Clare (A.D. 1253) was a saintly lady who laid aside her wealth and became a lowly follower of S. Francis, seeking poverty, spirituality, and Communion with GOD. She was appointed Abbess Sister of the poor at Assisi. She fasted very strictly and wore simple clothing, a tunic and cloth cloak, and walked barefoot. One day the Saracens besieged Assisi, when the saint held before the sacrilegious hosts a monstrance, beholding which the heathens fled abashed. This incident caused her emblem to be a monstrance, as in Perugino's painting in the Church of S. Cosimato at Rome, and in Lucio Massari's painting in the Bologna Gallery. Molanus places the Blessed Sacrament at her hand. A lily is sometimes given as her symbol, and in a French engraving she appears trampling on a scimitar and holding a tall fixed cross in a turban in the ground, in memory of her victory over the Saracens.

S. Rosa of Lima (A.D. 1617) was of the Spanish race, and was the firstfruits of the canonized saints of America. She was born at Lima, in Peru, and grew up a very beautiful child and woman. She took S. Catherine of Siena as her model, and loved to practise the most rigid asceticism and self-denial. One day her mother placed a garland of roses on her head ; the saint secretly inserted a pin into the wreath in order to give herself pain and cure herself of any feeling of vanity. This incident artists have loved to depict. In a painting in the Pitti Gallery, by Carlo Dolci, she has this rose garland on her head, and Murillo painted her crowned with thorns and holding a rose, on which is a figure of the Saviour. The infant Saviour in a nosegay of flowers, a crown of thorns, and a rose in her hand, are her most appropriate symbols.

SS. Justina and Cyprian were martyrs in the year A.D. 304. The English Calendar seems to have confused this S. Cyprian with the Archbishop of Carthage, whose feast day occurs on the 16th of September. This saint was surnamed "The Magician," a native of Antioch, a small town between Syria and Arabia. He practised magical arts, and hesitated at no crime, committing secret murders and attempting to assail the chastity of virgins. S. Justina was a beautiful maid beloved by a pagan nobleman, who summoned the aid of Cyprian in order to overcome her chastity. His arts were of no avail against the virgin, who repelled the attempts by the sign of the Holy Cross. This led to the conversion of Cyprian, and they shared together the pain of martyrdom during the Diocletian Persecution. She was scourged and he was torn with iron hooks and subsequently beheaded. Artists have, however, depicted a different death, and give as S. Cyprian's emblems a gridiron and a sword, and an old engraving shows him being burned in a pan with S. Justina. Callot depicts him burning his books of magic. S. Justina usually bears a palm. Bondicino places a unicorn at her feet, and B. Montagna depicts a sword in her breast. She is also shown vanquishing the devil by a cross, and a lily, the token of purity, is sometimes given as her emblem.

S. Faith was a martyr of the fourth century. This holy woman was very beautiful, and was martyred under Da-

cian, Prefect of Gaul. She was questioned
by the Prefect, who strove to turn her
from her Faith, and she was condemned,
like S. Laurence, to suffer on a brazen
gridiron, and then to be beheaded. A
sword and gridiron are her emblems, as
on a brass at Newton, Northamptonshire.
A window at Winchester Cathedral shows
her resting one hand on an iron bed. At
S. Laurence's Church, Norwich, she appears seated and crowned, with her iron
bed and book, and sometimes she has a
bundle of rods in her hand.

S. Bridget (A.D. 1373) belonged to the
Royal Family of Sweden. At an early
age she saw in a vision CHRIST crucified,
and the remembrance of this always caused
her to weep. She married, and after her
husband's death went on a pilgrimage to
Compostella. She lived a very severe and
ascetic life. Every Friday she would drop
burning wax on her naked arm, as depicted
by Callot. She entered a nunnery, and
then visited Rome and Jerusalem, dying

*Plate* 35.

Fra Bartolommeo]　　　　　　　　　[Alinari, Photo.

S. BRIDGET.

(See page 148.)

at the former city in 1373. A pilgrim's
equipment are her usual emblems, staff,
wallet, and bottle. On an English rood-
screen she is represented crowned, with
a crosier, book, and chain in her hand.
Sometimes she holds a heart marked with
a cross, and the Saviour appears to her
bearing the instruments of His Passion.
You may see her kneeling before a crucifix, or holding it in her hand, driving away
Satan.

S. Theresa (A.D. 1582), Virgin and
Abbess, was born at Avila, in Spain. Her
life was one of extreme spirituality and
communion with GOD. She joined a Carmelite nunnery at her native place, and
there she saw heavenly visions, the Saviour
even appearing to her. She restored the
spirituality of the rule of her Order. A
pen and a book are her usual symbols; in
addition to these an angel stands by her
with an arrow and a heart, alluding to the
legend of an angel appearing to her and
piercing her heart with a fiery dart, as is

depicted in a painting in the Louvre. A dove is sometimes seen flying to her, or hovering over her. Rubens painted her pleading for the souls in Purgatory, and in the Louvre there is a picture of her crowned with thorns, and having near the instruments of the Passion. A flame-crowned heart impressed with the sacred monogram, a crucifix, with a lily, are other emblems.

S. Hedwiges (A.D. 1242), the Patroness of Poland, was the daughter of Count Berchthold of the Tyrol, and the aunt of S. Elizabeth of Hungary. After the death of her husband she entered the Cistercian nunnery at Trebnicz, which she had founded. She practised most severe dis-cipline, and was very devout. She used to wash and kiss the feet of lepers, and never wearied in her devotion. Her piety and self-denial have inspired several artists. She is shown washing the feet of the poor, walking barefoot ; her shoes in her hand, and carrying the image of the Virgin and

infant Saviour.   In the *Die Attribute* she
is shown having laid aside the crown and
mantle of a princess, and attired in a nun's
robe.

S. Etheldreda (A.D. 679) is one of the
most prominent of our English saints.  She
married an Earldorman of the South Girvii
or Fenmen, and received the Isle of Ely as
her dowry.  She married her second husband,
Egfrid, afterwards King of Northumbria,
and following the call to the religious
life, she left her court and retired to the
lonely isle, and there founded a monastery,
of which she was abbess.  S. Wilfrid aided
her in her plans.   The saintly queen died
in 679.  Some years later her body, placed
in a marble sarcophagus, was translated to
the Saxon church.   Part of her shrine
remains in the beautiful cathedral.  She
appears in one of the bosses of the roof
of the choir.   She is usually represented
crowned, carrying a crozier and a book,
and frequently appears with these emblems
on several English rood-screens.   A saucer

with a crown of flowers or a budded staff are also her symbols. She is represented at Ely asleep, with a tree blossoming over her, and in the Benedictional of S. Ethelwold she has a book in her right hand and a lily in her left.

S. Ursula, a British maiden, with her companions, have been honoured for many ages with extraordinary devotion. She and her company left Britain when the pagan Saxons came, intending to settle in Brittany. Driven by storms across the northern sea, their vessel was sailing up the Rhine, when it was attacked by the Huns, and all were slain. The number of maidens was said to be 11,000 ; but this was doubtless an error for xi. M.V. (eleven martyrs and virgins). The martyrdom of S. Ursula has been a favourite subject for artists. On some English rood-screens she appears with an arrow or arrows in her hand, and her attendant virgins beneath her mantle. A choir window at Winchester Cathedral has a similar representation. An arrow is her usual emblem. A white banner with a red cross also sometimes appears. On the seal of the Drapers' Company, London, S. Ursula appears with a triple crown, sceptre, and palm, her mantle protecting her companions. The vessel on which she embarked is also sometimes shown, and in *Das Passional* she appears in a ship with a pope, bishop, and other ecclesiastics, and is shot at by an archer from the shore.

S. Winifred is a Welsh saint of the seventh century. She was the daughter of a soldier named Teuyth. A pathetic story is told of her. One day her father was worshipping with S. Beuno in a little church, when Winifred stayed at home in order to prepare something that was necessary for the Mass. Then a powerful prince came to the house, requesting drink, and was smitten by her charms. She repulsed him and fled towards the church, but the prince rode after her and cut off her head. A spring of water

*Plate* 36.

V. Carpaccio]      [Brogi, Photo.

MARTYRDOM OF S. URSULA.

(See page 153.)

sprang up where the ground was stained with blood, and the water of S. Winifred's Well is still said to possess healing qualities. Some accounts state that she was restored to life, and the prince, cursed by S. Beuno, died. On a Ringwood brass she is represented carrying her head severed from her body.

S. Gertrude died in 1292. This holy Virgin entered the Benedictine Abbey of Rodersdorff, Halberstadt, in her fifth year. All through her life she showed the greatest devotion and spirituality. For forty years she was abbess. She wrote a book on the *Insinuations of Divine Piety*, and records her conversion to God in her twenty-sixth year. As the end of her life approached, her visions of God increased. She beheld the loving Heart of God smiling on her in the guise of a garden full of spiritual delight. As the Litany of the Saints was being said S. John and other Apostles graced her fingers with rings. In art she is represented with these seven rings on the fingers of her right hand, and a heart with the figure of the Saviour in her left.

S. Elizabeth (A.D. 1231) has been the subject of many poems, and frequently is represented in art. The daughter of Andrew, King of Hungary, and wife of the Landgrave, Lewis of Hesse, S. Elizabeth was a model of charity and patience. Her almsgiving was unbounded. Her husband ordered her not to bestow so much charity on the poor. Meeting her one day carrying in her apron some loaves, he asked her what she was bearing. She said that her apron contained flowers, and when he demanded to see them she unfolded her apron, and the loaves had been changed to roses. Her charity and good works are often commemorated. Holbein painted her giving clothing to a crippled child, and other artists have loved to depict her benevolence. Sometimes she wears a double or triple crown or three crowns. There is a statue of the saint at Marbourg

Cathedral representing her crowned and
holding a church.   A basket of bread and
a flagon of wine are also emblems of her
charity.   Fra Angelico painted her with
roses in her robe, and she sometimes appears holding a basket of the same flowers.

S. Cecilia (A.D. 220), Patron of Musi-
cians, was of noble Roman birth, and was
betrothed to Valerian.   On her wedding
night she told him that she had a guardian
angel who would protect her virginity.
Valerian respected her confession, but,
demanding to see the angel, he was
directed to Pope Urban, who, on account
of the persecution, was hiding in the Catacombs.   Urban bade him return to his
house, and there he heard divine music,
and saw a radiant angel beside his wife,
bearing two garlands of roses.   Torture
and death awaited the devout lovers.
Valerian was beheaded, and Cecilia scalded
in her bath.   She survived this torture,
and suffered little hurt, but was subsequently beheaded.   She has been a favourite

subject with artists. Her love of music has supplied her usual emblem, organ-pipes in her hand, as in Raphael's painting in the Bologna Gallery, or a harp or violin. She has many other symbols, amongst which may be mentioned a crown, a wreath of roses in her hand or on her head, a palm, a sword, a sprig of almond-leaves, white roses and lilies, three wounds in her neck. In the church dedicated to the saint at Rome she is seen reposing in her tomb, and Cimabue painted her seated with a palm and a book. In the catalogue of saints she appears being boiled in a cauldron, and Gueffier depicts her showing an angel to Valerian.

S. Bibiana (A.D. 363) was born at Rome during the great persecution instigated by the Emperor Julian. A church is dedicated to her at Rome, and a dagger and a palm are assigned her as emblems, though it was said that she was beaten to death with plummets of lead. Sometimes she has a branch of a tree in her hand.

S. Lucy (A.D. 304) was a native of Syracuse, of which she is the patron saint. She accompanied her mother to the tomb of S. Agatha in Catania, in order that her mother might be cured through the virtue of that saint. S. Agatha appeared to her in a vision, and prophesied that she should be a virgin devoted to GOD, her mother healed, and that Lucy should bestow honour on Syracuse, and attain to her own saintliness. On returning to Syracuse her betrothed, discovering her resolve to maintain her virginity, accused her of being a Christian. She was imprisoned in a house of ill-fame, and was subsequently blinded, and finally slain by the thrust of a sword in her throat. She is represented with her eyes in a dish or on a book, or as presenting them to the Blessed Virgin Mary. A sword through her neck, or held in both hands, a dagger or poignard, a pair of pincers, are also her symbols.

## CHAPTER XIII

### *The Seven Champions of Christendom*

THE prosperity of nations in the ages of faith seemed to be permanently secured if they were placed under the immediate tutelary protection of a patron saint. To him prayers were addressed for the weal of the nation. He was the invisible guardian of its army. His name, invoked in the national battle-cry, "S. George of England," "S. Denis of France," infused courage and ardour into the soldiers who fought under their banners. By the consent of tradition there have been seven chosen champions of Christendom who have guided and guarded the destinies of the nations of which they were the patron saints. These are

M

S. Denis of France, S. Anthony of Italy,
S. James of Spain, S. George of England,
S. Andrew of Scotland, S. Patrick of
Ireland, and S. David of Wales. The
stories and legends of the lives of some
of these have already been given. Some
record of the other champions are here
appended.

The memory of the Patron Saint of
France, S. Denis (A.D. 272), is greatly
venerated in that country. He was
sent on a mission to Gaul by Pope
Clement, and founded the sees of Paris,
Chartres, and others. His companions
were SS. Eleutherius and Rusticus. Such
progress did they make in converting the
people of Gaul that the anger of the
Roman Emperor was aroused. A Roman
Consul was sent to Paris, and the three
saints were ordered to be beheaded. Our
Saviour appeared to S. Denis on the eve
of his martyrdom and gave to him the
Holy Eucharist. His martyrdom is the
subject of most of the representations of

Plate 37.

S. ANTHONY AND S. GEORGE. (See pages 76 and 164.)

the saint, and he is usually depicted carrying his head in his hands. In the Church of S. Denis at Paris there is a representation of the saint wearing a mitre and bound to a cruciform tree, two mallets lying on the ground. He is believed to have carried his head to Montmartre, where a church was erected in the seventh century. His relics were conveyed to the abbey, where now stands the beautiful church of S. Denis, the burial-place of the kings of France. Throughout France there are very numerous representations of the saint with his usual emblem, a sword or an axe.

The Patron Saint of England is S. George, who was martyred in A.D. 303. In the Diocletian persecution a young Christian soldier of Nicomedia[1] tore down the imperial edicts which ordered the torture of Christians and the destruction of churches, and for his act was roasted at a slow fire, the stern composure with

---

[1] S. George was born at Lydda about 270 A.D.

which he bore his suffering astonishing
and mortifying his executioners. This
holy martyr must not be confounded with
George of Cappadocia, the Arian Bishop
of Alexandria, the successor of S. Athanasius in A.D. 356, a persecutor of the
orthodox Christians who raged against
Catholics of every class, and by his
exactions became no less odious to the
pagans than he was to the orthodox. He
was massacred by the populace on Christ-
mas Eve, A.D. 361. However, legends
have confused the two, and some of the
events in the life of the heretical bishop
were attributed to the brave soldier-
martyr.[1] Bede states that the martyr was

[1] "We have had two S. Georges in history, and,
to our shame, we have made them one; and the
while we have borne his banner, the red cross, into
every corner of the globe, have placed his badge on
the noblest breasts, have kept his day as our special
feast, have given his name to the most regal chapel
in our land, have dedicated to him one hundred and
sixty-two churches; and while we have been doing all
these things in his honour, we have been indolently

beheaded under Dacian, King of Persia. The story of his slaying the dragon came later. The popularity of the saint in England dates from the Crusades; at the Council of Oxford in 1222, his feast was ordered to be kept as a national festival, and when Edward III founded the Order of the Garter, S. George became the patron saint of the kingdom. He is also the protector of Genoa and Venice, and his name is revered in all the Oriental Churches. No saint is more famous in art. We see him in every guise standing in armour piercing a dragon with a spear which has a cross and banner at its top, riding on horseback tilting at the dragon. His white banner with a red cross is his frequent symbol, and a sword instead of a spear

content to allow our greatest historical writer (Gibbon) to describe him as one of the lowest scamps and darkest villains that ever stained this earth with crime."

*Hepworth Dixon.*

is sometimes his weapon. Before him falls the idol of Apollo in one representation. Giorgione's finest work of the storm at sea shows S. Mark with S. George and S. Nicholas going in a vessel to aid Venice. The saint appears in Andrea Mantegna's picture of SS. Michael and George now in the Louvre, and in countless other paintings, being ever associated with the Archangel in slaying the dragon, the emblem of sin and Satan. On coins too he is often represented, and his figure is engraved on armour, as on a suit in the Tower of London, given by the Emperor Maximilian to Henry VIII.

S. Andrew of Scotland and also of Russia, the first-called Apostle of our LORD, is often mentioned in the Gospels. The scenes of his missionary labours were Scythia, Cappadocia, and Bithynia. Some account of his life and martyrdom has already been given (p. 37).

S. David of Wales was of noble descent.

His father, Prince Sandda, dreamed that he would receive three gifts—a stag, a fish, and a swarm of bees. The honey denoted the son's future sanctity, the fish his abstinence, and the stag his power over the old serpent, as stags were believed to devour snakes. S. David founded twelve monasteries and lived a holy austere life, converting the wild Welsh tribes to the Christian Faith. On the banks of the crystal Honthy he fed on leeks; hence Welshmen wear leeks on his festival. S. David's Cathedral and Diocese preserve his name. Scenes from his life appear in the mosaics at the east end of the church. The brass of his shrine remains, though the *feretrum* has been destroyed.

S. Patrick of Ireland, Bishop and Confessor, drave out snakes from the Emerald Isle, and has for his symbol a snake. His life has been often written, the two earliest being recorded in the famous Book of Armagh, of the seventh century. He founded the Cathedral Church of Armagh

in A.D. 445, and many other churches;
and, as Angus the Culdee sings—

> "Seven times fifty cleric bishops
>    The saint ordained,
> With three hundred pure priests,
>    Upon whom he conferred orders."

We have already given some account
of S. James the Greater, the champion
saint of Spain, and his connection with
that country, which has also for its patron
S. Isidore, Bishop of Seville (died A.D.
636), whose emblem is an angel holding
a plough while the saint prays.

S. Anthony of Padua is the champion
and patron saint of Italy. Some account
of his life and of his numerous emblems
which artists have loved to bestow upon
him has already been given (p. 76).

## CHAPTER XIV

### *Saints who have inspired Art*

NO saint has been more frequently
represented in art than S. Sebastian.
He was martyred in the year A.D. 287.
A citizen of Narbonne, and a favourite
of Diocletian, he was made commander
of the Praetorian Guards. Under the
military cloak he proved himself a true
soldier of CHRIST, and consoled the
martyrs in their trials, urging them to
stand firm. He was at length betrayed
to the Emperor, who ordered him to be
led to an open plain and shot at by
soldiers as a target. His wounded body
was discovered by Irene, the widow of
Castulus, who had also been martyred.
Again he bore witness to the truth, and
denied that the Christians were enemies

Plate 38.

Pollaiolo]                    [Anderson, Photo.

S. SEBASTIAN.   (See page 170.)

of the Emperor or the State. Diocletian ordered him to be flogged to death, and his body cast into the Cloaca Maxima. The corpse of the brave martyr was, however, rescued and buried in the Catacombs. Artists have loved to depict the tragedy, and have bestowed upon it all their skill. The saint is usually represented naked, bound to a tree and pierced by arrows. Belluci painted a picture of him accompanied by Faith and Charity. Giovanni Benvenuto, or Dell' Ortolano, depicts him together with SS. Roch and Demetrius. Antonio Pollaiuolo painted a noble picture of the martyrdom with figures of his executioners discharging their arrows. In the Vatican there is a painting on this subject by Pinturicchio, and in the Uffizi Gallery, Florence, Giovanni Bazzi, styled Il Sodoma, depicts the martyrdom and shows an angel descending to crown the saint. He appears also in the " San Sebastiano " of Titian, and in the " Madonna and Saints," by Giovanni Bellini. Many other examples might be given.

S. Valentine, whose feast-day occurs on February 14th, has somehow come to be regarded as the patron saint of lovers. He was a faithful priest, and for his zeal suffered persecution. He restored the sight of the young daughter of his stern judge, whose eyes by this miracle were opened to the sacred light of the Gospel. Hence the sun sometimes appears as his symbol. He was beheaded outside the Porta del Populo, at Rome, formerly called the Porta Valentini ; hence a sword is his usual symbol.

Very numerous are the representations of S. Nicholas of Myra (A.D. 342), the patron saint of mariners. Some poor scholars came to Athens, and were murdered by their hosts, their bodies being cast into a tub. The saint convicted the murderers and restored the dead to life. The legends of S. Nicholas have provided many subjects for artists, and appear in glass and painting and carved in stone. The font at Winchester Cathedral shows some scenes from his life. The three youths whom he rescued are often shown emerging from a tub or chest or kneeling before him. Three golden balls upon a book are often his emblems, as in the paintings of Botticelli, Gaetano Bianchi, and others at Rome. Andrea del Sarto places the three balls in his hand. His charity to the three poor maidens whom he rescued from a life of ill-fame is shown in the painting of Fra Angelico, in which the saint is depicted handing money through a window. He appears in his episcopal robes, and an anchor, a ship, and a model of a church are other of his emblems.

The charitable act of S. Martin of dividing his cloak with a poor man has been seized upon by many artists, and appears in numerous paintings. The incident occurred outside the gate of Amiens, where stood an old man bare of

*Plate* 39.

Capanna Puccio]          [Anderson, Photo.

S. MARTIN. (See page 174.)

clothing, begging. Martin, who was a young soldier, not yet baptized, had nothing to give save his cloak ; so, drawing his sword, he cut it in twain, and gave one half to the beggar. He is usually shown on horseback, dressed in a white cloak. Van Dyck's painting at Winchester Cathedral depicts the scene, also Molanus, Caxton's Golden Legend, some old tapestry of the Vintner's Company, London, and numerous other works of art in Western Europe show this charitable act. CHRIST appeared to him clad in the portion of the cloak, saying, " Martin, yet a catechumen, has covered Me with this garment." He was elected Bishop of Tours, and founded a monastery. His courage in opposing the Emperor Maximus and the conduct of the Spanish bishops in their treatment of the heretic Priscillian, is remarkable. The devil oft tried to tempt him, but he resisted with the same brave spirit.

S. Christopher was very popular among

the painters of our English mural decorations, as the sight of him was deemed to preserve a man from danger during the day. He is always depicted as a giant, and the legends attached to him are well known. He set out on his pilgrimage to find the most powerful prince on earth. We need not follow his adventures until at length he was baptized by a hermit, and set to carry travellers over a river. The Infant CHRIST appeared to him, convinced him that he was bearing the Creator of the world on his shoulders, and caused his staff, planted in the ground, to flower like a palm-tree. He was ultimately martyred. He is usually represented as a giant wading through a river with a growing tree in his hand, and carrying the Infant Saviour on his shoulders. On the river-bank you can usually see his lonely hermit's cell.

S. Leonard often appears in art. He lived in France in the time of the Visigoths, and is the patron saint of Limoges. He is also the patron saint of prisoners, and loved

N

to release them from their fetters, according to the Old English rhyme :

" But Leonard of his prisoners doth the bandes
        asunder pull,
    And breakes the prison doores and chaines wherwith his church is full."

The Prince of Antioch, Bohemond, son of Robert Guiscard, when he came to France in 1106, visited Limoges, and offered silver fetters to the saint's altar for his escape from captivity. He is often represented in art releasing prisoners from the stocks. On our English rood-screens he appears with chains or manacles with a lock, sometimes with chains and a crozier. Broken fetters, an ox lying with him, holding a youth by a chain who is mounting a ladder, are some emblems of the saint. Andrea del Sarto (Viennese Gallery) painted him with fetters in his hand, and in an engraving in Camden's *Britannica* he appears holding a vane.

There are many other saints whose lives

and attributes we should like to recall to the memory of our readers. But these must suffice. Many lessons can be drawn from their constancy, their courage, their simple faith. The storms of persecution may again rage to try our strength. By lesser trials and more insidious ways is the Christian's faith now proved. Whether all the legends recorded be true or not it is needless to inquire : they proclaim the ideals of Christian fortitude, perseverance, and courage, and teach lessons which are not unprofitable to the followers of CHRIST in every age.

"*Justorum animae in manu Dei sunt, et non tanget illos tormentum malitiae : visi sunt oculis insipientium mori, illi autem sunt in pace, Alleluia.*"

LAUS DEO.

# INDEXES

## I

### *Saints with their Symbols*

Aaron.—Censer or rod, 6.

Abraham.—Knife, 5.

Adrian and Natalia, SS.—Lion's head at feet, 70.

Agapetus, S.—73.

Agatha, S. — Breasts on dish ; pincers ; veil, 128, 129, 160.

Aldhelm, S.—Harp, 81.

Alphege, S.—87.

Ambrose, S.—Scourge and crown ; tower ; beehive, 115, 116.

Amos.—Shepherd with sheep, 6.

Amphibalus, S.—79.

Symbols of St Agnes.

St Andrew's Cross

Agnes, S. — Lamb ; dove bearing ring, 126, 128.

Aidan, S.—Stag ; lighted torch, 74, 87.

Alban, S. — Sword and cross, 79, 80.

Andrew, S.—**X** or **V**-shaped cross ; fish-hook, 22, 24, 37, 162, 167.

Anicetus, S.—Wheel, 94.

Anne, S. — Triple crown and book, 15, 18, 19.

181

Anselm, S.—Ship, 83.

The Hog & Bell of St. Anthony.

Anthony, S. (Hermit).—Hog, or goat, 75, 121.
Anthony of Padua, S.—Book; lily, 76, 161, 169.

Pincers and Tooth. St. Appolonia.

Apollonia, S.—Pincers holding tooth, 130.

Athanasius.—Pallium; heretics beneath feet, 120, 121, 165.
Augustine of Hippo, S.—Inflamed heart with arrow; eagle, 115–117, 133.

Barnabas, S.—Stone; or flames and stake, 62, 65.

Sᵗ Bartholomew.

Bartholomew, S.—Flaying knife; knife and book, 22, 24, 38.
Bede, Ven.—Pitcher, 84.

St. Benedict · A raven & a broken sieve

Benedict, S.—Raven and broken sieve, 97, 98.
Bernard, S.—Three mitres at feet; beehive; white dog, 98, 100–103.

St. Catherines Wheel studded with knives and broken

St Bruno

A Crucifix

Sᵗ Callixtus: a mill-stone

St Cecilia : an Organ

The Vase of
S.<sup>T</sup> MARY MAGDALENE

*Anchor and Ship
Symbols of S.<sup>T</sup> Nicholas*

St Norbert

A Chalice

Swords of St Paul
in the Arms of
St Paul's Cathedral

Raven & Palm
Symbols of St Paul the first hermit

The Keys of St Peter
in the Arms of Exeter

A knife　　A Sword　　A palm branch

St. Peter Martyr

# II

## Symbols of the Saints

Anchor.—S. Clement, 67.
   ,,   S. Nicholas, 174.
Angel.—Malachi, 6.
Angel holding plough.—
S. James the Great, 169.
Angel with arrow and
heart.—S. Theresa, 150.
Angel with man's face.—
S. Matthew, 49.
Apples.—S. Dorothy, 130.
Ark.—Noah, 5.
Arrow.—S. Giles, 122, 125.
Arrow (sometimes con-
joined with sceptre or
globe).—S. Edmund, 85.
Arrow, body pierced by.
—S. Sebastian, 172.
Arrows in hand.—S. Ur-
sula, 153.
Axe or sword.—S. Denis,
164.

Balls, three golden, on
book or in hand. — S.
Nicholas, 174.
Banner, white, and red
cross.—S. George, 166.

Basket of bread, or
flowers, and flagon of
wine. — S. Elizabeth of
Hungary, 158.
Basket with bread. — S.
Philip, 33.
Battle-axe.—S. Matthew,
52.
Battle-axe.—S. Matthias,
24, 42.
Beehive.—S. Ambrose, 116.
   ,,   S. Bernard, 102.
Bier.—S. Lazarus, 61.
Boat.—S. Jude, 37.
   ,,   S. Lazarus, 61.
   ,,   S. Martha, 60.
Boathook.—S. Jude, 37.
Book.—S. Bartholomew, 38.
   ,,   S. Paul, 26.
Book and arrow.—S. Giles,
125.
Book and lily.—S. Anthony
of Padua, 77.
Book, cross, and rosary.
—S. Dominic, 108.
Book of Sarum Use in
hand.—S. Osmund, 89.

192

O

Printed by A. R. Mowbray & Co. Ltd.
London and Oxford